BIRDS OF THE
AFRICAN WATERSIDE

By the same Authors

BIRDS OF THE AFRICAN BUSH

BIRDS OF THE AFRICAN WATERSIDE

Paintings by
RÉNA FENNESSY

Text by
LESLIE BROWN

COLLINS
St James's Place, London
1979

To Dennis and Michael Fennessy; and to Robin,

from his Toastwatcher, with affection:

William Collins Sons & Co Ltd
London · Glasgow · Sydney · Auckland
Toronto · Johannesburg

First published 1979
Book design and illustrations Réna M Fennessy 1979
Text Leslie H Brown 1979

ISBN   0 00 216 079 X

Set in Garamond 156 and 201
Printed and Bound by Poligrafici Calderara,
Bologna, Italy

Contents

Acknowledgements

The Artist wishes to express her thanks to the late Sir William Collins, who conceived the idea of this book, to the Trustees and Director of the Kenya National Museum who made it possible by kindly loaning specimens, and to Alec Forbes-Watson, ornithologist, for his help and advice in producing the pictures.

Both artist and author are deeply indebted to Barbara Brown for her constant support and for typing the manuscript, and to Peter Squelch for all his invaluable assistance and encouragement.

Introduction

Some years ago there was a popular song in America about water. It conjured up visions of a parched land in which the thirsty cowboy (or outlaw) longed for the shade of 'that big green tree where the water runs free'; and ended each verse with someone twanging a guitar and intoning almost ritually 'cool-clear-water (waudr)'. It may have been trite but it rang true. And, Oh! how true in Africa! We live in a car-borne age now; but I am old enough to remember foot-slogging across the scorching plains at midday, aiming for a long line of big green trees where I knew that water, that blessed 'cool-clear-water' ran free, where I could plunge, or at least slosh it over my body with my hat; and in an instant feel a new man, refreshed, invigorated, enlivened.

Water is life; without it none can exist. Waterless places are called deserts because they are deserted. The water may only be a small bitter trickle from a spring in the midst of barren desert hills; but there you may find a Common Sandpiper on migration, and 10,000 sandgrouse will collect to drink from 5000 miles around, the males even taking water in their absorbent breast feathers to thirsty young far out in the desert itself. Where water abounds there life abounds, especially when it is not cold. A big tropical river or the shore of a tropical lake seethes with life, bird life included. There are water plants, lush, succulent and always green; among them water insects, crustaceans, and such nastier things as leeches and mosquito larvae; small fish and frogs to eat these, and birds and bigger fish to eat the small fish and frogs. At the top of the aquatic food chain are large predatory fish; otters, Fish Eagles, tall herons, pelicans, and majestic storks, among the most impressive birds in the world.

Even when the water itself is nasty – and it is *very* nasty in some alkaline lakes – life may abound in it. Probably the greatest of all bird spectacles is at Lake Nakuru in East Africa where, in their unpredictable fancy a million or more Lesser Flamingos – the 'little red water nymphs' *Phoeniconaias minor* – may gather. Hundreds of thousands may collect in pink masses together, like a field of exotic flowers; and each one is clean and neat, despite the foul fluid in which they live. These huge hordes survive on the blue-green algae growing in abundance in water that would kill any animal foolish enough to drink much of it, extracting, by filtering with their specialised bills, as much fodder as a first-class pasture can produce. That is really what it is – greenstuff growing in nutrient-rich water; but among birds only the flamingos can effectively harvest it with their specially adapted beaks. Other birds that live at Lake Nakuru harvest a surplus of small crustacea, or recently introduced small fish – all algae eaters too – Great White Pelicans, pompous and important looking on the ground, majestic in soaring flight, take about 2500 tons of fish per year (500lb/acre) from Lake Nakuru without noticeably diminishing the supply.

Birds of the African Waterside

This gives some idea of the abundance of waterside life. And often, one can sit in a chair or in a boat and watch it all in comfort with little effort, and the proverbial bottle of iced beer handy. The waterside can also be grilling hot, and the sun trying as it is reflected from the wavelets. It can be fly-ridden; and the water itself can carry nasty diseases, such as Bilharzia (a very unpleasant waterborne disease, found where humans live alongside water snails), or breed malaria-bearing mosquitoes. But watersides are more often delightful places, presenting a huge variety of scenery, and supporting a bewildering variety of birds frequently both numerous and confiding, so that watching them is not a difficult pastime. Surprisingly, anyone who does so will find that little is known about even common species; I have mentioned a few of the mysteries in the pages that follow.

Our fresh water all, originally, comes from the sea; and much of it makes its way back there eventually. But some is taken by mountains from the winds in their eternal sweep over the earth. Mountains, it has been said, should not be asked to produce anything but water; or rather, catch it from the wind and deliver it safely lower down, where we can use it for drinking, bathing, irrigating or making electric power. If we interfere with the primary water-producing function of mountains we shall soon suffer – and are suffering deeply now – from the consequences of our folly in violent floods or landslides; muddy streams that dry to a trickle in the dry season and become raging torrents in the wet; and a variety of other ills and sorrows that could be prevented if we only left alone the mountainsides and the forests that often cover them.

Our story of the African waterside begins here, sometimes on the big mountains of East Africa and Cameroon, more often on lesser mountains and among little hills still big enough to catch some water from the wind. On a few big East African mountains it begins as water from melting snow and ice, as it usually does in the northern mountains, or the Himalaya and Andes. However, most tropical mountains are not that high; and very often the water begins as little trickling streams among ferns, moss and bamboos, shaded by big trees. The little trickles join to produce bigger streams further down, where one may sit on a boulder encrusted with the shelly spraints of *Aonyx*, the clawless otter which eats crabs and mussels and watch birds in the big trees round about. Many years ago, in Trinidad, I used to make my way up such little mountain streams and lie naked above a clear pool on a log, whistling to call up birds that I would otherwise never have seen. Many a time since in Africa I've had the same glorious sense of solitude and peace in the cool forest shade. But if one leaves the water and walks into the forest gloom one can soon be lost, and be glad to find one's way back once again to the banks of the life-giving element.

Some such little streams, that ran from the once wild and uninhabited little hills of the Nigerian bush, are unforgettable to me. I was usually hunting, or at least wandering about with a gun and binoculars in days when that did not seem so great a crime as I'm told it does now. After a hard fifteen mile round in the morning, with my faithful Hausa henchman Momo – the finest African and one of the finest men I've ever known – we used to seek shade towards midday and perhaps find a little trickling stream in a *kurimi* on a hillside where we would rest and chew the fat until the descending sun relented enough to let us start on our homeward way. Here were Blue Fairy Flycatchers, exquisite, aptly named little birds; and the sweet songs of Snowy-capped Robin Chats to beguile the hours. Once, dead beat after a gruelling day measuring rice crops, I crossed such a little stream in the moonlight. I had already crossed it earlier that day, and found it muddy and uninviting after a night's rain. Now it ran more gently, magically silver between banks of inky trees. I sat and bathed my tired body in it, listening to the sweet whistling call of a forest nightjar, and the deep ominous grunting of a Verreaux's Eagle Owl. Then I went on my way, strengthened and refreshed.

The water of the little streams runs on downhill, joined by other little streams; slows as it reaches flatter ground; and stills into long pools separated by rapid riffles. The river here may be fifty to a hundred yards across, and even in the dry season, when one knows it is free of bilharzia, one still does not cross it lightly. They tell me that most crocodiles are harmless, but there are odd ones that are not, and I confess that when I've had to swim such a river to get from A to B I've done it with my heart in my mouth. The same water that seemed so kindly and refreshing higher up the hill here carries an element of menace. Monkeys and apes are bad swimmers and cannot or dare not cross such a big river too wide to be spanned by a fallen tree; and perhaps that elemental fear of theirs comes out in me. Giraffes, ostriches and some other big animals that apparently could easily wade it won't cross either. Others, such as waterbuck and elephants, even lions, swim it without thinking. And of course it's no barrier to most birds.

Unless humans live near it – which they all too often do these days – any such river provides the charm of deep cool quiet shade along its banks. In open plains, where shade is scanty and often thorny, those big green trees lead one to coolness and water. How pleasant to come in from the open bush in the dry season and camp here, where at midday one may watch brilliant kingfishers, bee-eaters, and rollers hawking insects; herons, egrets and various plovers on the sandbanks; may catch a passable fish for dinner; and at night sit by the fire of flood-borne dry logs and listen to owls calling, lions roaring, hippos burbling, and the trumpeting and crashing of the great elephants coming to bathe with as much evident pleasure as any human being shows. If you are lucky the electrifying grunt of a leopard walking along a stone bed may crudely punctuate the night with fear, acknowledged by the barking of baboons and the deep crowing of colobus monkeys.

In flood, such biggish, fast-running streams can be terrifying. They can come with a rush and a roar from far away, where you saw the lightning last night against the sky; sometimes just as a deeper rumbling in the midst of a perfect starlit night. I once lunched, alone, on a rock with a little fig tree on it in the bed of the Daua river in Ethiopia. The torrent was coming down brown and roaring, and to reach my tree I jumped a small channel. As I ate I realised that the angry roar of the river in white water over the rocks at the head of the rapid had grown silent; and that it had risen two feet, quietly and with infinite menace. Fortunately the channel I had jumped was narrow, though much deeper now; and thereafter I could pick my way from stone to stone where twenty minutes earlier I had walked across dry sand. If I had not subconsciously paid attention to the voice of the water I should not be writing this now, for I could not have lived through the maelstrom in a gorge below my chosen rock and tree.

The really big rivers, the Niger, the Nile, the Congo and especially the Zambezi are titanic in their power in flood. At the bottom of the Zambezi gorge, below Victoria Falls, the surge of an eddy throws whitecaps several feet up a bank of stones, to come suddenly licking at your feet. In a small swift dug-out canoe one may take an hour's hard paddling to cross the Niger or Benue, and a little bit of bank showing above the brown swirling flood where in the dry season a thirty-foot clay cliff towers proves that the river is moving with stupendous power. In the dry season the same river alternates with huge clear pools a mile long, riffles thigh-deep over sandy beds and golden sandbanks half a mile or more across, the haunt and breeding ground of Skimmers, terns, Egyptian Plovers and pratincoles. Or braided rapids may meander among rocky islands clothed in forest, where the hippos doze contentedly in back-water pools.

I have made many safaris on the Niger, *Sanders of the River* style, sometimes for a month or more on end. Then watching the birds of the sandbanks was my principal amusement; and before the sun grew too hot and the sand scorched my bare feet I used to disembark from my canoe and race it to the next embarkation point upstream, finding nests of various birds on the way. The Egyptian Plovers and Grey Pratincoles – delightful little birds combining in their flight characteristics of the tern, the swallow, and the blown leaf – did broken-wing acts before me, and the Skimmers buzzed me when I cae too close to their nests. Then I would re-embark, to paddle along some huge pool, maybe thirty feet deep, over which Rosy Bee-eaters flighted, and where kingfishers of several sorts perched on roots of big trees sticking out of the banks, or fishermen's netpoles.

Birds of the African Waterside

At night, when I camped, I chose a sandbank in the middle of the river, where there were often friendly river people, who spent their lives in huge canoes, with a brass-knobbed Victorian bedstead and frilly pillows in the stern for the master and his wife. One such evening I was due to contact a colleague, each of us about two hundred miles from home on our mutual border. I saw his launch proceeding down a deeper passage while my canoe took a shallower route. I put a shot across his bows in the traditional manner; and we dined together on a sandbank, and afterwards listened to his records of 'Eine Kleine Nachtmusik', to the accompaniment of real crickets and frogs, in a setting Mozart could never have imagined but which seemed perfect to us.

Many rivers end, or at least pause, in lakes, big or small. The biggest of African lakes are inland seas, with islands and beaches and breakers, some deep and clear as crystal like Lake Tanganyika, others shallow and opaque with silt brought down by inflowing streams, which may make them richer in life if not too dirty. They support an incredible variety of fish – there are over 2000 species in Africa, compared to about 200 in Europe; and a great variety of fish-eating birds to eat these fish. These vary from the majestic Goliath Heron, that could kill a man with its bayonet beak, to small cormorants, Little Bitterns, Pied Kingfishers, grebes and Darters. Their ways of catching fish by stealth, surprise, co-operation, hovering and unique trigger mechanism of the Darter are endlessly fascinating. Sit at the edge of a lake such as Lake Naivasha and it is all laid out in front of you. Over all flies the Fish Eagle, whose melodious yell at dawn is one of the best-loved sounds in Africa. The Fish Eagle may not only itself catch fish with beautiful dexterity but can rob even the biggest of other fishing birds, the Goliath Heron and Great White Pelican, of what they have caught. It is not above robbing a Pied Kingfisher of a fingerling that can only be a snack to the eagle, or pirating a catch from its own offspring or mate.

Then there are all those other water birds, ducks and geese, rails, coots, ibis and plovers that either feed among the waterside reeds or probe in the mud. In winter swarms of European and Asian migrants waders pour into Africa, and those who think of a ruff as a rare bird in Holland may see five thousand together on the shores of Lake Abiata in Ethopia. The richest of all waterside environments is where a freshwater river pours into an alkaline lake, creating an intermingling of habitats and species. Even the Lesser Flamingo likes fresh water in which to drink and to bathe; and one may easily see more than fifty species of water birds in a day in such a place.

If a lake is alkaline it is because it has no surface or subterranean outlet. The water runs in, carrying with it dissolved salts. The sun shines, sometimes with great heat, and the water evaporates, leaving the salts behind. Sometimes the very springs feeding such a lake are themselves strongly alkaline and that seemingly nice clear water is bitter and undrinkable; or it may even be boiling hot, killing any vegetation near it. Over millennia such lakes shrink by degrees, and become more and more alkaline; two in East Africa are crusted with solid soda. The more alkaline the lake, the fewer the species of fish. In Lake Tanganyika, a huge fjord-like expanse of clear water which in places is so deep that the bottom is thousands of feet below sea level, there are about 125 species and 42 genera of fish that occur nowhere else; yet it is hard to buy a good-sized fish on the shores of Lake Tanganyika, which has only one small outlet. Lake Rudolf, now called Lake Turkana, has far fewer species of fish, but they are often very abundant, and include huge behemoths of Nile Perch. The shallow, weed-grown lagoons along the shores of Lake Turkana are full of water birds, but the steep and gravelly or stony shores of Lake Tanganyika are almost devoid of even common species.

Other big lakes may have many sizeable rivers running into them and a very big one running out. Lake Victoria, the biggest of all in surface area, gives rise to the Victoria Nile. Now it goes through turbines, as Winston Churchill forecast. Lower down it becomes a majestic rushing river, almost a mile wide, tearing its way down towards the Murchison Falls among rocks and rapids. One thinks of the Nile as old; but here it is young, as a river goes, and that is why it is so rough and boisterous. On the rocky islands in midstream there are patches of unspoiled forest; and White-collared Pratincoles rest and nest on black water-worn rocks, safe from all interference.

Big rivers develop a floodplain in their lower course. When in flood the channel, which is usually higher than the adjacent plain, becomes too small to hold all the water, and it bursts out sideways, maybe as far as eight or ten miles wide on either side, and fills this floodplain. The plants that grow there must be able to withstand this temporary inundation, and usually forests on higher ridges alternate with stretches of long, stiff-stemmed grass that in the dry season is burned to black ash. However, green shoots soon provide abundant food for big animals, such as buffalo, lechwe, waterbuck, kob and puku. Other big animals move in flood to adjacent high ground if they can; if they cannot they will die out. Floodplains of this sort are tremendously productive; but they very often have heavy human populations living near them so that the adjacent habitat is ruined.

In due time the flood recedes; and then in old courses of the river, in oxbow lakes, the water that ran brown and muddy a month or so before stills and becomes clear. Water lilies and other such plants spread out over the surface of these little lakes, and provide habitat for a myriad of waterbirds, from the mighty Saddle-billed Stork to brilliant gallinules and the long toed Jacana that walks Agag-like across the leaves themselves. Migrant ducks, Pintails, Garganey, and others, in the northern winter join the resident species, ranging from the huge, rather ungainly Spurwing Goose to the White-faced Tree Duck or Whistling Teal – *wishi-wishi* as the Hausa call it after its sibilant call – and, nicest of all, the diminutive Pygmy Goose, which is often local and rather hard to see.

Such floodplains are generally hot, humid, malarious regions devoid of much attraction unless they are uninhabited by humans. I have spent a great deal of time slogging over floodplains, with the day temperature over a hundred and the nights not far short; and I have generally found them uninviting. I cannot forget the mosquitoes of the Niger floodplain in March, that bit like dogs through the seat of one's canvas chair, and paid no attention to repellents. But occasionally, even in a floodplain, one can find an enchanted spot.

There was one such, on a tributary of the Kaduna River in Nigeria, a place called Umo-Umo, though what that meant I never found out. Two days' trek from the nearest railway station, and further still from a road, I found it on my way homeward from a hunting trip. I stayed only three or four nights – all the time I could spare – sleeping on a rocky knoll above a clear blue lake, with a view up and down the plain. The little lake was alive with birds and full of fish; and beyond it was a screen of figs and big Acacias on the river bank levee. In the vertical ten-foot banks of the river itself were colonies of Carmine and Red-throated Bee-eaters, and Senegal Thickknees nested under shady bushes on the sandbanks exposed between trickles of clear water. I was out hunting each morning, but in the evenings used to walk along the river bank to surprise bushbuck, and would see the herds of bright rufous kob grazing in the open. Towards dusk I sat in my deckchair looking over the water; and at night, when I woke to throw another log on the fire (for I slept in the open without a tent, and there were hyenas about) it seemed as though I was all alone in the wildest of wild Africa. Actually I had a cook, Momo, and about fifteen porters along; but they were all replete and slept soundly fifty yards away so that they did not disturb me.

That was long ago, in 1943; and I have often wondered what sort of hell the human race has made of the place since. Probably it is now densely populated, a stinking, fly-infested market, with the little lake fouled with disease and transistors at night instead of the eerie whistling of the Thickknees. Probably it would be unwise to go back; but one may still find such places where tsetse fly or some other barrier keeps most humans away.

More recently, in Ethiopia, I have found other enchanted watersides. My brother was for some years warden of the budding Omo Valley Park, and he made his headquarters above a clear tributary, the Mwi. Below his house on a cliff was a deep clear pool, in which we bathed night and morning; you could drink in the water as you swam if you wished. In the short space of a few years since then it has become infected with Bilharzia. Small crocs lived in the pool;

Birds of the African Waterside

but all the big and potentially dangerous ones had been shot by my brother, who gained added satisfaction by naming them after Socialist Cabinet Ministers. Wilson and Castle took the knock quite early, and their belly skins were not even made into fancy handbags but into concrete carriers. He never got Callaghan, who lived in a deep pool upstream and could hide in long reeds. The few small and cowardly crocs in our bathing pool were known as back-benchers and presented no real risk.

I used to wander up the stonebeds of an evening, alternately stepping dryshod over shallow clear riffles and poking cautiously through thickets under giant figs, where pied Colobus Monkeys gazed idly at me, spreadeagled at ease over the huge yellow limbs of the figs. I have never seen such a place for kingfishers. Seven varieties frequented the river bed, the Giant, Pied, Woodland, Grey-headed, Half-collared, Malachite and Pygmy; and an eighth, the Striped, lived in the savanna nearby. The clear pools swarmed with small barbel, alas uneatable because of their needle-sharp bones; and they supported some of the kingfishers (some were insectivorous), eight species of herons, and at least three of storks. There were Fish Eagles by day; and at night Pel's Fishing Owl. We first knew the owls were there when we heard a sonorous hoot we could not identify; and we later found their roosting places in among the forests of big figs. Like most owls they had regular roosts, and we could always locate them. However, I never stayed out late enough to watch the owls fishing, for the thickets flanking the river crawled with buffalo, and though I'm not ordinarily afraid of buffalo any of these might have had a poacher's bullet in him and so borne a grudge against even well-meaning mankind. So I used to return before dark; and at night when I woke I would hear the owls hooting up and down river, and Senegal Thickknees whistling; and sometimes an old buffalo, whom we called 'Ferdinand' after the Disney singing cartoon because of his habit of warbling in his bath, came and splashed in the pool below the house.

I met Pel's Owl again in Botswana, in the Okavango Swamps where we lived on an island a hundred miles upstream from Maun and made a film about Fish Eagles. It was not the best place to make a film of Fish Eagles; but it was another enchanted spot. I slept outside, under huge ebony trees, and in the cold clear night I used to wake; listen to the gentle chuckle of the river flowing over roots and stumps; maybe thrill at a lion's roar, turn over, and say to myself 'Having a good night's sleep; may as well go on with it!' At dawn I was woken by the song of Robin Chats while it was still almost dark; and the strange rattling call of the Crested Barbet. Then we breakfasted, and took a boat to go and work on the Fish Eagles.

In the evenings it was my job to go and catch fish to feed the eagles, who used to form up as soon as they heard the outboard coming. As it grew dusk I went back up the clear broad stream where in still stretches the sunset colours of the sky were thrown back, and herons and egrets flapped to their roosts. The swamps were alive with birds, not always easy to see. Pygmy Geese were more abundant than anywhere I have known them; and there was a beautiful coucal, the Coppery-tailed, which lived in the tall reeds, and a rail of some sort, probably a flufftail, that called and called but remained invisible.

Soon after this I began working in earnest on the diurnal behaviour of Fish Eagles at Lake Naivasha. By then I knew the lake well; and my plan was to sleep in my boat, start watching chosen pairs at dawn, and keep watching them all day to see how often they caught fish. I set out on a rough evening, and ate my dinner by the light of the moon in a little lagoon where the waves did not rock my boat. When they quieted I set out across the open lake; and alone on the water, with the great mountains of the Riftwall standing up all round, the works of man, exemplified by the twinkling lights of Naivasha and a train grinding along the railway, seemed small indeed. One could see why the flamingos, which passed overhead invisible but calling to each other on their way to Lake Magadi paid no attention to such little pinpricks on their nocturnal environment. I reached my chosen lagoon and went to bed to the tintinnabulation of a million tree frogs; the nasal toots of coots and galinules showed that they also were busy. A chorus of Swamp Warblers wakened me well before dawn.

Introduction

So, although watersides have sometimes been hot and unhealthy, they generally have been for me places of delight, because of the birds and beasts I saw there, and sometimes the fish I caught. If I had my choice of the infinite variety of watersides I have known in which to live which would I choose? Maybe the almost magical freshwater spring at Mugun, at the north end of Lake Hannington (now called Bogoria) beneath the frowning Ngendalel escarpment, where one can sit in a cool clear bath and watch a pageant of Lesser Flamingos watering at the spring and nearby geysers; but maybe the smell of sulphur would get me down. Or it might be a small remote island in Lake Victoria, with a resident pair of Fish Eagles; but that might become limited in time. I suspect that if I could really choose, and could find a place of the sort outside a National Park where I could do what I liked, I would pick a knoll above a floodplain, such as that at Umo-Umo, with a clear lake, a good-sized river, and lots of big animals as well as birds; and plenty of tsetse and mosquitoes to keep human beings and their livestock away. One must make sacrifices somewhere for peace.

Wherever it was, whether on a lake where I could get about mostly by boat, or on a riverside where I would make quiet paths through the thickets to surprise and watch forest animals and birds as well as those of the waterside, it would abound with life, of a variety and beauty beyond compare, born of the abundance that springs from the water itself.

BIRDS OF THE AFRICAN WATERSIDE

1 The Mountain Wagtail
Motacilla clara

Wagtails are among the nicest of small birds. Their svelte forms, with that continually wagging tail, and their clear and pleasant colours mark them out. They seem much more attractive than most of the dull and difficult pipits that are their nearest relatives. Some wagtails, notably the Pied Wagtail, often make their homes with man; and I can remember them singing to me on my Nigerian verandah as I dawdled away the hours of the hot tropical afternoon. Wagtails are beautiful; entirely harmless, because they live on insects; and evocative of the spirit of chattering mountain streams. What fisherman has not enjoyed the company of a wagtail as he cast his way quietly upstream?

Most of the wagtails in Africa are migrant yellow wagtails from Europe; but there are three resident species, the Pied, which is found round any houses, and is liked as a bird of good omen by African tribes; the Cape Wagtail, which in Lesotho is a bird of mountain streams, but in Kenya prefers swampy places and papyrus beds; and the Mountain, or Long-tailed Wagtail (if you live in South Africa) which is always a bird of mountain streams, and of all is the most closely associated with watersides. All three are beautiful; but to my mind the neat grey, white and black plumage of the Mountain Wagtail is more attractive than the Pied, or the duller Cape Wagtail. Perhaps it is not quite as attractive as the European Grey Wagtail, also a bird of mountain streams; but that is a matter of opinion.

We may like a bird because of itself or because of the places and times when one meets it. In the Mountain Wagtail I would have to admit that there's a large element of association, for I have come to know it best when trout fishing on Kenya's highland streams, flowing through forests then alive with buffalo and rhinoceros – which did not worry me but kept other intruders away. Here, as I moved slowly along the banks, casting my fly at intervals, or sitting idle in the shade when the fish were off the take, I was seldom out of view of Mountain Wagtails. Pairs kept to their own stretches of river; and as I worked upstream or down so they would move in front of me, teetering with wagging tails on stones in midstream, perhaps singing a snatch, then flying on. Finally when they had reached the edge of their territory they

The Mountain Wagtail

flew back over my head with sharp cries before they trespassed. On many Kenya mountain streams there is a pair to about half a mile of river; and along this stretch they have their favourite spots where they are regularly to be seen. Such places are often shallow with mossy boulders in midstream; and not far away there may be a big rock, or a small overhung cliff where, in season, they will nest.

I have a pair on the stream below my house at Karen, and I can see them most days if I will. Their favourite place is a little waterfall gushing in white water over rocks, where there are small ferny islands and banks of watercress. I am always meaning to build them a rocky tower with a ferny nesting niche in it; but I never have. Alternatively, at midday, they like a quiet stretch just above this fall, where the deep shade of a huge old *Newtonia* tree and two of its vigorous offspring creates a quiet dark place where I like to pause and watch them. They will fly upstream from here another fifty yards; but there the stream emerges into more open ground with reeds, and they don't seem to like that; snakes, maybe. Although they have not trespassed on any other wagtail's stretch they turn back here and fly over my head down to the fall again.

This pair nests on a mossy ledge between two spouts of a waterfall about two hundred yards below my boundary; in a huge tree above this fall Crowned Eagles used to breed. I suppose they must sometimes succeed, but in the years I have known them they have not always nested and if they lay they often fail. This is partly why I have thought of making them a better place; but they might be perverse and not use it. So I keep an eye on the fall; and in September, the driest season, when the river has shrunk, I usually see some signs of new activity on the mossy remains of the old nest, perhaps almost washed away by the spray and soaking wet of April floods.

This nest site is similar to many I have found; but these wagtails in East Africa and Ethiopia may also breed on a ledge of a boulder in the middle of a big pool – there was one that I had to swim to examine; on a tree-stump sticking out of the water when low, stranded by some great flood many years before; or in a ledge of a small cliff where the water has undercut the rock and they are safe from all but a determined human being or perhaps a snake. I suppose their enemies may include Marsh Mongooses and serpents; but I do not know. In fact, although it would be so easy, and so pleasant, this is yet another of Africa's birds that have never been studied in great detail.

The nests are made of moss, gathered from the wet cliffs and boulders, and they are often used, or rebuilt in the same place, year after year. They are lined with fine rootlets; and soon after this lining has been placed in the cup two or three eggs, white but marked with grey and brown, are laid. The wagtail begins to sit when the clutch is complete; and the young hatch in about 14 days and are about 14 days in the nest. If the pair succeeds in rearing a brood the young wagtails, known by their somewhat shorter tails and somewhat less elegant plumage, accompany their parents from boulder to boulder for as much as two months. Then, one day, they are gone; and the familiar adults are once again left in undisputed posession of their stretch of river.

Length 7 inches, sexes alike

2   Black Duck
Anas sparsa

and Peters' Finfoot
Podica senegalensis

These two birds of wooded streams and rivers are none too easy to tell apart, for often all that one sees of either is a skulking form escaping downstream under bushes on the bank, emerging from the cover to slip away through the rapids of the pool tail and disappear. Knowing this habit, I once had the fortune to recognise a Finfoot in an area of south-west Ethiopia where the species was likely to occur but had never been recorded. It turned its head to look back at me as it escaped downstream; I had my binoculars fixed on it, and at once saw the white strip down the side of the neck and the long pointed bill. That Finfoot's curiosity or alarm made definite a record I would otherwise have been reluctant to claim.

The Black Duck is, on the whole, much easier to see than the Finfoot; and when in doubt one ought to say 'Black Duck', rather than give rein to one's imagination. In East Africa it is to be found on most highland streams within forest, but if the forest has been cleared it may still be found, and readily flies up and down stream of an evening. It occurs on tiny alpine tarns on Mount Kenya, up to 14,000 feet; but in South Africa can be found at near sea level, along streams running through forest not unlike that on East African mountains. It is nowhere very common, and almost always occurs in pairs, each pair on a particular stretch of river. I have never seen a flock of Black Ducks, though I have seen more than two together and supposed they were parents and the survivors of their brood.

Black Ducks are not really black, but dark-coloured, with the lower back and wings spotted with white, and a greenish-blue wing speculum between white bands. Fishing for

trout on mountain streams of an evening I have become aware of them as they land with a splash on the quiet waters of a big pool, often to take off again at once with an alarmed quack when I made another cast. Sometimes, too, when I have been sitting quietly on the bank, they have swum downstream towards me, unaware; or, on searching mountain heights I have seen a pair of dark forms in the middle of a little shallow alpine tarn, or sometimes startled one out of the tussock grass on the bank of such a place. Search as I may, I have never found a nest, though I have seen some broods of ducklings. From this we know that in East Africa the Black Duck breeds mainly in the drier seasons of the year, which seems sound because its nest with eggs close to the waterside is then less likely to be flooded out. Food supply, which one may suppose is perennially abundant along streamsides, probably has little to do with it.

Black Ducks have been studied intensively in South Africa by Roy Siegfried and others. They breed on small islands in the middle of streams, or on the banks where there are rushes, occasionally in holes in trees. Like many other ducks they lay a large clutch of buff-coloured eggs which are incubated by the female only, though the male remains not far away. The eggs hatch in about 32 days and the ducklings, brown marked with black, at once take to the water, and thereafter remain with their parents till they can fly well. The broods are reduced by enemies of one sort and another, probably mainly predatory mammals rather than birds; but enough survive to keep a small population going. While no long-term harm is done by shooting an occasional Black Duck to eat anyone who thinks that they can be shot in numbers is wrong; the population is far too small to stand any heavy shooting. Not for nothing has the

Black Duck and Peters' Finfoot

name *sparsa*, meaning scarce, been bestowed on this duck, which is confined to African watersides, and to only certain types of these in the higher parts of the continent. Quite possibly the total population is not more than a few thousand pairs.

Finfoots may look like but are not ducks, or even related to them; they are members of an aberrant family placed between rails and cranes, and found elsewhere only in the tropical East and South America. Although harder to see than Black Ducks on highland streams they are more adaptable, and widespread, frequenting any quiet stream with forested banks, big rivers, and sometimes the wooded shores of lakes. I have seen them alike on the tropical Ogun river in Nigeria and at 5500 feet on forested Kenya streams. They too can usually be found about the same stretch of river; but one very seldom catches this bird unawares. The best way to see one is to approach the river very quietly and then sit in deep shade on the banks. If you are lucky a Finfoot may appear, swimming low in the water, and resembling a Merganser or Goosander more than anything else in its general behaviour. It will probably perceive you at once, no matter how still you sit, and dive or scuttle over the surface for a few yards, later sinking in the water and hurrying away downstream. Finfoots scarcely ever fly any distance – or no one has seen them do it; and although they are said to give a loud screaming call I have never heard one utter a sound.

I have only once seen a Finfoot at really close quarters and out of the water, and then I was so flabbergasted that I did not take full advantage of the moment. It was a female – more brightly coloured than the male – right out on the bank, near a tree stump carried down by floods and covered with flood debris. I could see her bright red feet, which she placed deliberately as she stepped towards the water, jerking her tail up and down as she moved, in the manner of rails. She looked so unlike any other Finfoot I ever saw (and I had not seen many others up till then) that I could not for the life of me think what she was. It occurred to me that I ought to go and search in the flood debris; but she was thirty yards from me on the opposite bank of a deep and swift river not far above a waterfall, and I was bound for another appointment. When I looked the bird up in the book I concluded it was a female Finfoot; and thought; 'Oh blast! In that case there might have been a nest.' I was probably right, for the nest of the Finfoot, at that time unknown, was later found in just such a place, among piles of flood debris. Discovery perhaps missed by a hairbreadth; or rather through lack of time and the depth of the river between us. Yet, I do not really mind, as the memory of that queer creature stepping about on the dry stalks like a cross between a duck and a moorhen remains clear, and revealed more about the relationships of the Finfoot than any other view I ever had.

The Finfoot is still very little known. Even its food is obscure, though it presumably eats frogs and water insects. Only a few nests have ever been found, one in Kenya in a bank behind roots about five feet above water. It contained two olive brown eggs, marked with darker brown, which agrees with the few other descriptions known. If anyone wants to study a really *difficult* bird, a real challenge, this is it. It would be best observed by quietly skulking along selected river banks. In fact, behaving rather like a Finfoot oneself.

The Black Duck, length 19 inches, sexes alike
The Peters' Finfoot, length 18 to 21 inches, male larger

3   The White-starred Bush Robin
Pogonocichla stellata

This exquisite little bird is not really a bird of the water itself, and may indeed be found far from water inside deep forests. However, there is no better place to get a good view of it than a forested river bank, where it may occasionally emerge right into the open among the roots of a big tree, or even hop out on to a stone standing in the water. Only then can one truly appreciate the beauty of its colouring, for, although it looks brightly coloured in a museum drawer or in a painting, inside the forest and in the deepest shade near the ground it practically disappears. The olive green of its back affords near-perfect camouflage from the rear while the bright yellow of the underparts is somehow inconspicuous in shade. But in the sun, on a river bank, it is a jewel.

White-starred Bush Robins are common in Kenya highland forests and thus may be observed with patience by anyone who works his way quietly along a stream. In South Africa they occur at lower altitudes, almost down to sea-level, in the forests of Natal and Knysna. One gets to know how common they are when one knows the calls – an essential key to learning almost anything about skulking species of the forest undergrowth. The normal call is a mournful subdued whistle, 'Hu-wee-ter-terr', repeated many times; and this may be followed by a rattling call almost like a low growl. These noises are made by males displaying to one another, when they may square up a few feet apart, raising the otherwise quite inconspicuous white eyebrow, and displaying the white spot on the throat. They may allow close approach when they are thus engaged and, as they show off their yellow undersides and golden upper tail coverts their mutual antagonism resembles that of Robin Chats rather than anything else.

They also utter these calls when alarmed; and as soon as one enters the territory of a pair they start calling. If they are fairly close by, within twenty yards or so, one may then sit down and stay quiet; and in a few minutes the calling stops, and they go about their business as before. They feed chiefly on the forest floor, perching a few feet above it on the branch of some low shrub, and making short flights to catch some insect among the leaves. They are often in attendance on the marching armies of driver ants that disturb insects in the forest litter, and make them fly straight into the mouths of agile little birds.

The White-starred Bush Robin

Although the White-starred Bush Robin is so common, and when one knows its call not too difficult to watch, finding its nest is another matter altogether. I suspect that one could do so by systematic observation of a pair in their chosen haunts; but most of those I have found have been located by chance. The first was at the base of a small tree between buttressed roots. The bird flew off when I was within three feet or so, revealing two eggs. Unfortunately, the nest was despoiled by a predator that very night, and I was never certain to what it belonged as I had only had a vision of a dull greenish or brownish back as the sitting bird left.

Another year my wife and I were watching a pair of Black Sparrowhawks in the forest opposite our house, and by then I had some clues as to what to look for, as I had several times found on the forest floor curious collections of dead leaves which could not have got there by chance, and from one of which I disturbed a White-starred Robin. Beside the track to the Sparrowhawk's nest, among grass tussocks, I found another nest, and watched it through most of the cycle. Sitting quietly in the forest, watching the wary hawks, I found another, with three eggs, by seeing the Robin go down to a likely patch of grass and remain there. This one came to grief, but the other hatched safely – although, one wet night, an outsize male leopard passed within a few feet, slipping and sliding as he came down the track.

No doubt the sitting Robin never stirred for him, any more than he or she did for us. We could stop on the path, and then approach cautiously to within five feet of her; and all we could see was a little white spot on either side of the head, the beak and a bit of dull olive-green back in the half-domed nest. These markings actually helped to conceal the sitting bird rather than otherwise, breaking up what outline there was.

This nest, like others I have found, was a marvellous construction calculated to look like a chance mass of dead leaves on the forest floor. In the centre of the leaves there was a mossy cup; and in this two eggs, with a blueish ground half obscured with pale brown spots, forming a zone at the broad end. You had to know it was there before you could see the nest or the sitting bird at all, for the entrance was shaded by a tussock of low grass. Luckily I found it at an early stage of incubation, and watched it, not very seriously, till the young left. The eggs hatched in 16 days and the young flew in another two weeks. I never watched for long spells, and afterwards regretted it, for a quick search through the recent literature did not reveal that this Robin had ever been deeply studied in South Africa, as I assumed it must have been. Another occasion when a little more work looking at the literature first would have made a chance to observe and record more worth-while.

Since then I have found one nest, in a hole in a tree about two feet above ground. White-starred Robins will also use nest boxes, and one nests in a friend's greenhouse among the orchids. Their secretive ways make them always difficult to observe; and they are not seen in their full beauty in the depth of the forest habitat, but only occasionally when they flit out briefly on to the edge of a river to catch an insect, and thus rarely expose themselves to the light of the sun.

Length 6 inches, sexes alike

4 Pel's Fishing Owl
Scotopelia peli

One does not expect owls to catch fish, somehow; it seems out of character. Yet in Africa and the far East there are several species of owls of the genera *Scotopelia* and *Ketupa* which live almost entirely on fish. Like Fish Eagles and Ospreys their feet are equipped with rough spicules on the soles of the toes to help in grasping their slippery prey; and since the fish presumably cannot hear the owl's approach and take evading action they have dispensed with the soft, sound-deadening feathers of most fully nocturnal owls.

In West African forests there are two other species of fishing owl, the Rufous and Vermiculated, both belonging to the same genus *Scotopelia*. Their nests have never been found, like those of so many forest owls. Pel's Fishing Owl is more widespread, and occurs along wooded stream banks in savanna or even dry thornbush, as well as in forest. Evidently, it is the wooded stream bank that matters, not the type of country around. When more is known about these fishing owls it may be found that Pel's is a savanna species which does not like real rain forest, while the other two are true rain-forest species. Knowing Pel's Fishing Owl well, I could not find it along rivers flowing through forest in South-western Ethiopia, though it was as common as anywhere I know on rivers in savanna not very far away.

My first acquaintance with this owl was memorable, if unpleasant. I was on one of those long slogging foot safaris in the Niger flood plain, and camped by a little river not far from Agenebode, whose chief was certainly among the sublimest of potentates, for he was known as the 'Okunmagbe of Weppa-Wano'. He had no desire to make his people grow rice for the war effort; but I had been told to make him like the idea, and so there I was, camped beside this foul hot river investigating a particularly nasty-looking expanse of flat clay to see whether I could grow rice on it. It goes almost without saying that in a temperature of 100 in

the shade, at the end of a hard tour of duty, I was seized with a violent attack of malaria, which Mepacrine failed to control. I sent runners in two directions for a supply of natural quinine; and meantime lay on my bed and sweated. The place was one which no ornithologist had visited; and rather than leave it entirely uninvestigated I sent my henchman Momo out with two cartridges to see what he could find. He returned with a Pel's Owl and a Tiger Bittern *Tigriornis leucolopha*, a rare species of heron. No collector can ever have secured a better right and left; but he had entirely blown off the owl's head at close range, so we were only able to identify it by the wing feathers.

    I saw no more till I went to the Mwi River in Ethiopia. There, my brother and I heard sonorous hoots at night which we knew belonged to no owl we had heard before; and it could only be Pel's. Search later revealed their roosting place in a clump of small forest trees. When disturbed one of the owls flew up on to the branch of a big Acacia, in full sun and broad daylight, and sat there blinking, evidently not much incommoded by daylight. Thereafter we always found them there, and learned that there were a pair of these owls for every three or four miles of the river bed. We learned little else about them, because we never found a nest at any time I was there, and never watched them hunting. Although said by some experts to be largely diurnal, I have always found Pel's Owl wholly nocturnal. Once we disturbed one of the owls sitting on a stump in the evening above a pool; but they were usually on their roosts till towards dusk. I confess I was too afraid of the buffalo and crocodiles to walk the Mwi stonebeds by night to see whether I could catch the owls at their fishing.

    One hellspot and two enchanted watersides are associated for me with Pel's Owl, the last being an island in the Okavango swamps. I guessed the owls were there by finding a feather;

Pel's Fishing Owl

and not long afterwards I heard that telltale deep hoot – 'Hooommm' – pause – 'Hut', which can actually be a duet. One night the pair came and duetted on a dead stump a few feet above the clear water; and left only when I rose and shone a torch on them to establish their identity. I could not find them by day among the islands; but on a moonlight night they came again and duetted on a dead tree for twenty minutes, in full view of five people. They were filmed by Dieter Plage with a light intensifying device; and they only fell silent when we played their own calls back to them on a tape recorder.

Again, I found them entirely nocturnal here; they were never on the move or audible by day. Since then their habits have been studied in greater detail in this part of Botswana by Tim Liversege; his results have yet to be published. The recent Tana River expedition to Kenya was asked to keep a look-out for them as they went downstream. They found them in several places, and actually filmed them catching catfish, themselves attracted to the maggots in the putrefying carcase of a stranded elephant. Catfish swim deep by day but often surface at night, so perhaps are important prey for Pel's Owl.

So, perhaps by the time this is in print, Pel's Owl will not be quite the mysterious bird it has been to me, and was even more so when Momo brought me that decapitated carcase many years ago. For me the unforgettable times were those when I skulked quietly through the thickets of the Mwi riverside, never quite sure what I would come upon, to locate the owls in the same grove of trees evening after evening, and watch them, drawing closer and closer till they finally took wing and flew a hundred yards or more to other groves, their plumage seeming unnaturally bright orange-brown in the evening sun. Their great dark eyes looked down at me, unafraid until they finally could stand no more and left. I am sorry I did not stay up to watch them on moonlit nights; but I might not even have seen them, and there were other things to be done. One cannot work hard all day and then stay up watching all night – not even for Pel's Owl.

Length 25 inches, sexes alike

5   The Shining Blue Kingfisher
Alcedo quadribrachys

Some kingfishers catch fish; others, perhaps the majority, live on insects, crabs, frogs, lizards, even small snakes. Some eat no fish and live in the depths of forest, not on riversides at all. Those that eat fish are brilliantly blue, reflecting the sunlit blue water in which they hunt, while those that eat insects are bigger but duller coloured. The only exception to this general rule (among African Kingfishers at least) is the Pied Kingfisher, which is black and white; breeds in colonies in banks; and in addition is the only kingfisher which regularly hovers over open water.

The Shining Blue Kingfisher is the most brilliantly blue of all the African Kingfishers and is exclusively aquatic, though whether it entirely confines its diet to fish is not absolutely clear. It is said also to eat crabs. It is a rare bird in East Africa, for its main haunts are within the equatorial forest, where it frequents small streams and the wooded backwaters of the greater rivers. Here it perches, often in shade, watching for fish; and may often be seen when it takes wing, startled perhaps by a passing canoe, shooting like a streak of brilliant cobalt light across or along the stream, to alight again on another perch in the shade and almost disappearing once the sun leaves its plumage. Less often one may see it perched right in the open, and then there is no doubt of its identity, for it lacks the conspicuous crest of the almost equally beautiful Malachite Kingfisher, the blue of its back is darker and more intense and its beak is black. In flight the back and upper tail coverts are a lighter cobalt blue, shining brilliantly in the sun.

Its belly is chestnut; and one wonders whether this common colour scheme among fish-eating kingfishers – bright blue above and chestnut below – has anything to do with camouflaging them from a fish's vision. Such conundrums must occur to any enquiring naturalist; but how to solve them without being a fish oneself? All one can say is that the frankly insect-eating savanna kingfishers have little bright blue in their plumage, and lack chestnut undersides, while a 'dual purpose' type such as the Grey-headed Kingfisher, which eats both fish and insects, has a fair amount of bright blue *and* a chestnut belly. There is something in this; exactly what is not clear.

Shining Blue Kingfishers fish like any other small kingfisher of their type; that is, they perch motionless on a branch or the stem of a reed, intently watching the water. Seeing possible prey, they may bob their heads up and down, as if in excitement, but more probably to focus on the kill. Then a short swift dive, penetrating sometimes six inches below surface, and the little bird emerges again with a silver fingerling in its bill. Back to the perch, against which they hammer the fish mercilessly until it is subdued, then swallow it head first. Then, sit there, looking satisfied, again bobbing the head up and down. The rate of success for any fish-eating

The Shining Blue Kingfisher

African Kingfisher has not to my knowledge been expressed quantitatively by anyone, though someone may have done this statistical exercise for the European Kingfisher which is a close relative. However, it is probably fairly high. It would not be difficult for even a casual observer to collect figures of this sort.

If our Shining Blue Kingfisher, having caught its fish, does not at once swallow it but flies off like a streak carrying the fish along in its beak it probably has a nest. Like other fish-eating kingfishers it breeds in banks, digging its own nest hole. The difficulty is to make a start on the face of a smooth bank; and kingfishers do this by hurling themselves at the bank and jabbing with that powerful, pointed beak, which doubles as a pickaxe and a fish-spear. Once the beginning is made the kingfisher digs and digs, disappearing within and pushing out loose earth behind it when it emerges, so that a hole under construction has a tell-tale heap of fresh loose earth beneath it. At the end of the tunnel, which inclines slightly upwards, and in the case of the Shining Blue Kingfisher may be about two feet long, a round chamber is made in which the eggs are laid.

Kingfishers eggs are round, glossy and all white; and when fresh the contents show through pinkish, giving them a soft salmon flush. The Shining Blue Kingfisher lays four to six eggs at the end of its tunnel, but virtually nothing more is known about its nesting habits. In the Congo it is said to breed in October and December and in Uganda both in the dry month of February and in the rains, April and May. It is more likely to breed in river banks when the water is low, in the dry season or early rains; but there is not enough evidence to go on.

Probably, when more is known about this glorious little bird it will be found to behave like the European Kingfisher; that is, the nest hole must be dug afresh each year. Both sexes incubate for about 21 days. Both sexes feed the young after they hatch, though at first the female remains in the hole and the male brings food for her and the brood. The young grow up in a mess of their own droppings and fish bones, and leave the nest after 23 – 27 days. Malachite Kingfishers at least tend to rear a series of broods one after the other in the same hole; and quite likely this may happen with the Shining Blue Kingfisher also. Anyone who finds a hole can extend our knowledge by watching it; or, better still, digging a covered pit behind it and sitting therein, observing the comings and goings of the adults through a glass or perspex plate let into the back of the hole. The plate must be removable because the young inevitably foul it with their droppings. The technique has been used successfully for other hole-nesting birds, including bee-eaters and hornbills. Although Hilary Fry did not invent it, it is now known as 'doing a Fry'. It remains to be done with the Shining Blue Kingfisher, though it is unlikely that the bird in the hole will seem as beautiful as they do outside, flying across blue water in the brilliant tropical sun.

Length 5 inches, sexes alike

6 The Water Thickknee

Burhinus vermiculatus

Thickknees, so called because of their large 'knee' or tibiotarsal joints, are a strange family of birds occurring over most of Europe, Asia and Africa. The European species is known as the 'Stone Curlew', because it lives on stony heaths and calls at night a little like a Curlew. Neither it nor any other thickknee are actually closely related to Curlews; they are nearer to bustards and cranes. All thickknees are medium-sized, and are dull-coloured birds until you look at them closely, when the beauty of their finely barred and marked plumage becomes apparent. They are all largely nocturnal, which is probably why they have large, striking bright yellow eyes. A big head is needed to accommodate these big eyes; hence the South African name 'Dikkop' – thickhead. Some are inhabitants of open plains thornbush; others of watersides, where they frequent sandbanks and like shady places with dead leaves. Here they remain almost invisible, reluctant to move until one is within a few yards of them.

The Water Thickknee is one of those exclusively found near watersides, and very widespread in tropical and South Africa. It occurs from the Cape to Liberia; but in West Africa be careful to distinguish it from the Senegal Thickknee, a bird of almost exactly similar habits but which takes over as the dominant waterside thickknee from Senegal to Ethiopia, south to northern Uganda. The two can be distinguished only by a distinct white bar on the shoulder of the closed wing in the Water Thickknee; the Senegal Thickknee has none. Having seen both, and tried to understand their habits a little, I can perceive no other difference in their behaviour. Yet they manage to keep separate from one another, the Water Thickknee in West Africa being confined to the forested rivers and coastal areas while the Senegal Thickknee is

the common species of inland savanna, rivers and streams. In any place where both could occur, on the boundaries of their range, one would have to be very careful over identification; and it is very difficult to see that tell-tale white bar before the bird flies.

One sees little of thickknees by day. They then tend to rest in the shade of trees and bushes on sandbanks, but I know one pair of Water Thickknees which likes to rest in the blazing sun on top of a coral head at the mouth of Mida Creek on the Kenya coast. No doubt they feel safe there, surrounded by sea at all times except during the hour or two of low tide. By night, this pair of Water Thickknees comes to the shore, where they can be located by their sweet and mournful calling: 'Wheee-peee-peee-peee-peeee', in a descending cadence. It is hard to find out what they are doing then, because being a human one cannot see well oneself. However, the active parts of their lives takes place at night, and though many waterside or estuarine birds are active by night as well as by day thickknees are especially birds of the night. Sleeping on my roof, I often hear them calling to one another in the bay below my house; and it is a sound I love because it is associated with almost every good waterside camp I have had, anywhere in Africa.

I have not personally studied the breeding habits of Water Thickknees, but I expect they are similar to those of the Senegal Thickknee which I was able to study in Nigeria, since in every other respect their general habits appear almost identical. In East Africa, indeed, where the Senegal Thickknee does not occur, it is clear that the nests are placed in exactly the same sort of situation as those of the Senegal Thickknee, on sandbanks beside rivers or lakes or on

The Water Thickknee

the seashore, where they may nest on top of a coral head surrounded by surf. In Nigeria there were a pair of Senegal Thickknees to less than a mile of a small river I frequented, and I suppose that Water Thickknees would be about as numerous on any suitable stream in East Africa. One can determine this quite easily by hearing them calling at night; one pair is usually audible upstream, another downstream of one's camp.

Thickknees normally lay two big, regular oval eggs, stone in colour, with scrawls and markings of blackish brown and grey that camouflage them well against the sandbanks (or in England on a flinty heath) where they are laid. They would be much harder to find if the birds, relying on their own camouflage against enemies, did not very often sit tight till too late, leaving only when one has approached to within thirty yards or less. It is always worth looking where a thickknee comes out from under the shade of a bush on a sandbank, though the eggs are so well concealed that one must be very careful to avoid treading on them. For some reason or another, thickknees eggs always give me particular pleasure; they harmonise so perfectly with their sandy habitat.

Water Thickknees, and Senegal Thickknees too, must breed in the dry season along rivers, for the obvious reason that this is the only time that the nesting site is exposed and not in danger from floods. On islands in lakes such as Lake Victoria, where there is little danger from actual flooding, the season is more elastic; but here there is a sharp peak of laying at the end of the rains and beginning of the dry season, in September – October. In the Water and Senegal Thickknees both sexes incubate for about 17 days; when sitting they suffer from heat unless the nest is in the shade, which it often is. When one sees a thickknee alerted it appears frozen and rigid, as if made of stone. But from a hide at close quarters it loosens up beautifully, bobbing its head, looking around, and sometimes calling to its mate resting not far away. That big yellow eye is lovely.

After the eggs have hatched the young leave the site almost at once and run with their parents. Even when I knew where they must be I was seldom able to find the little chicks, so well are they camouflaged and so still do they lie until their parents indicate they can safely move. They stay with their parents, if they survive until they can fly, and if one sees three or four together it is probably a family party. Then they disperse, probably forced to do so once the rain and floods come, to find a vacant place along the river bed where one can join with a bereaved member of a pair. Such details are not known, though thickknees seem to have fascinated many people; and there is still much to learn. The trouble is that to understand them properly one should work at night, when any wild riverside is likely to be a slightly alarming place, with the crocs and the jumbos and the hippos barging about.

Length 14 to 15 inches, sexes alike

7 The Hadada Ibis

Bostrychia hagedash

My first meeting with a Hadada was one of those unforgettable moments of a bird-watcher's life. It was in Nigeria, and I was walking along the floodplain of the Oyun river near Ilorin, searching for guinea-fowl. On the branch of a big spreading Acacia not far from me sat a large brown bird. It allowed me to approach, closer and closer, regarding me curiously, apparently unafraid, until I was almost directly below it and no more than ten feet away. Then it gave tongue. 'Mwaaaa', it said; and again: 'Mwaaa-aaa-aa', in a raucous nasal braying tone, as it finally flew off in disgust. I have seen many Hadadas since; but never one that behaved quite like the first I met.

I often complain about the vagaries of systematists and in this case my complaint is that they have deprived this quaint and on the whole lovable bird of a far finer-sounding name than it used to have – *Hagedashia hagedash*, the perfect accompaniment, repeated with gnashing teeth, to hurling a plate against the wall or destroying a typewriter – both actions which have given me pleasure despite what they cost. The person who first thought of that must have had a sense of humour, I feel; and I'm sorry his imaginative work has been changed to the prosaic *Bostrychia*, which one can't enunciate with anything like the same ring. Hadada, or Ha-de-da, is obviously onomatopaeic for that extraordinary braying cry, uttered in alarm when the bird flies or when travelling to and from roosts at evening and morning. It becomes a familiar sound to anyone who camps along watersides, whether of streams, or lakes, for the Hadadas regularly fly along the river to chosen roosting places, and leave there soon after dawn to disperse to their feeding grounds. Several other species of Ibis, for instance the Ethiopian Wattled Ibis and the rare Green Ibis of mountain forests, utter similar far-carrying raucous calls; and the extraordinary rattling croaks emitted by a Wattled Ibis as it wakes up in the morning have to be heard to be believed.

Hadadas are actually among the least aquatic of African Ibis, normally feeding away from water, and not even necessarily in wet places. They like probing lawns and grassland with their long curved bills; and out in the open with the sun on them one can appreciate the iridescent beauty of the green patches on their wings. The sexes are hard to tell apart, and the pair normally stays together; but the male is slightly larger and has a longer bill than the female,

The Hadada Ibis

while in the breeding season it is likely that the bare patches of skin at the base of his beak are more brightly coloured than those of his spouse. Young birds have less iridescent green on the wings, and have shorter bills.

Hadadas are also more solitary than most ibis, feeding singly or in pairs, very seldom more than four together. In this they are more like the secretive Green Ibis of the forest than for instance the Wattled Ibis of Ethiopia, which usually goes about in flocks, but may on occasion be almost as solitary as a Hadada. When feeding they walk about sedately, probing here and there, eating large insects, snails and worms. They are probably completely harmless or actively beneficial, so that if one is lucky enough to have a pair about the garden they should be left alone, when they will often become quite tame.

The Hadada was the first of African Ibis to be studied in detail, by C. J. Skead, a well-known South African ornithologist who has contributed several notable life studies of individual bird species. They probably pair for the life of any individual, though the survivor of a pair will lose no time in getting a new mate. They have a territory in which they are regularly to be found feeding each day, and to which they fly noisily from the roost each morning and back again in the evening. Pairs roost together, flying off soon after dawn to go to their own ground. They nest singly, not in colonies; and the nest may not be near water at all, though it often is placed over water. I have seen one in a forest tree about as far from any water as that particular pair could breed.

The nests are flimsy structures of sticks, used only once, though another nest in the same general area may be made the following year. They lay normally two to four eggs, most often two or three, and these are rather beautiful for ibis eggs, pale bluish or greyish green, heavily marked with brown and red-brown blotches, sometimes almost covering the shell. They are laid at irregular intervals so that later on one may find young of several different ages in the same nest. In an equable tropical climate such as that of Lake Victoria Hadadas breed all the year round, but with a marked peak of laying in the early and main rains. This suggests that ground made softer for probing by rains is more likely to yield a rich food supply. In South Africa Skead found they laid mostly in September to November, with less widespread breeding than near the Equator.

Both sexes incubate for about 26 days, and when they change over there are no elaborate ceremonies. Each partner sits for several hours at a stretch and probably the female sits by night. The young when they hatch are unattractive, blackish and almost naked; and they remain unattractive for much of their time in the nest. They are fed by both parents by regurgitation, pushing their bills into that of the parent and receiving a mush of whatever the parent has been eating. They remain about 33 − 35 days in the nest, but at the end of that time can climb out on to branches. Nesting success is poor because many nests collapse and the young fall out of them. As in other such cases, this argues that Hadadas are quite long-lived birds. When the young leave the nest they accompany their parents for about two and a half months, and then go their own ways.

Length 30 inches, sexes alike

8 The Blue Fairy Flycatcher

Trochocercus longicauda

Although this lovely little creature is again not a water bird it is absolutely characteristic of the neighbourhood of small streams flowing through forest, even when these may be temporarily dry. It is also found away from water, but those who know it will associate it most with watersides. It is there, when one seeks shelter from the midday sun, and perhaps a cool pool where one can sluice the body with a sense of uttermost delight and relief even with muddy water, that one sees the Blue Fairy Flycatcher at its best. As one sits there, cooling off gratefully, it appears, flirting from branch to branch above the stream, perching briefly and spreading its tail vertically over the back while it droops its wings, darting about, never still. The Western African races are brighter blue and longer tailed than those in East and Central Africa, but have the same habits. The eastern races have been called prosaically 'Blue Flycatcher', as it is the only flycatcher which is almost entirely blue, with a white belly. But to me, who have so often seen its elegant form flitting about at close range in the deep shade of a streambed in Nigerian savannas, where the heat of midday sun a few yards away was well over three figures, the additional 'Fairy', bestowed by someone more fanciful or imaginative, whichever you prefer, is apt.

This little flycatcher used to be placed in a genus of its own, *Erannornis*, for there is no other quite like it. However, more recently it has been joined with the forest flycatchers of the genus *Trochocercus* which are themselves quite closely related to the Paradise Flycatcher, *Tchitrea*. In many of its ways it reminds me strongly of the Fantail Flycatchers *Leucocirca* which I knew as a boy in India, though these have even more elaborate tail-fanning displays. It does not sit still on a perch and dart out to catch an aerial flying insect as do many typical flycatchers, but is constantly on the move, actively seeking for its prey, caught either on the wing or under leaves where insects often try to hide. In this one can see its kinship with the Crested and even more beautiful Paradise Flycatchers; yet it is unique in its sky-blue colour and unusual tameness.

Despite the fact that it is widespread, from West Africa to western Kenya and south to Zambia and Malawi, it does not seem to have been studied by anyone in detail, though it sometimes breeds in gardens. It is yet another case of a common and beautiful bird which has escaped the attention of any enthusiast, though in North America or Europe it would have been sought out and observed fully. It even nests sometimes in gardens, and so should be

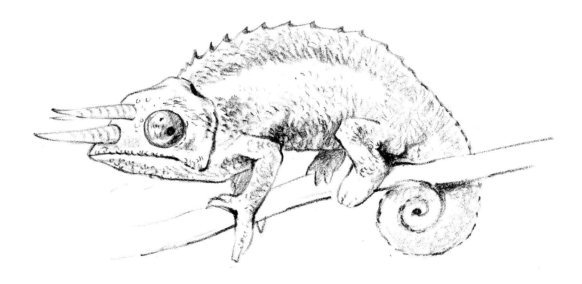

The Blue Fairy Flycatcher

within the reach of any competent housewife/bird-watcher minding the baby; and what a nice distraction it would be from the muling, puking infant with its messy nappies.

From what is known about it it is resident in its haunts all the year round. Probably each pair has a small territory of forest, usually a narrow strip along a small stream-bed, or a few acres of thicker riverside forest in which they may wander more freely. Pairs often move about together, constantly calling to one another with sharp little chirping cries; but the male also advertises himself in his territory by a twittering song, which is not remarkable but falls pleasantly on the ear. In a suitable place it is not long before one of the pair or both appears; and they have often seemed to me curious about the presence of a human being, returning again and again to have a closer look, sometimes approaching to within a few feet. Perhaps they take us for some kind of large monkey or baboon, which might help to disturb from among the leafs the small insects on which they feed. Certainly they, like so many other insectivorous birds, take advantage of the insect-flushing ability of the driver ants.

The nest, quite hard to find, befits the beauty of the bird. It is an exquisitely-made cup of fibres, adorned outside with grey lichens, bound with cobwebs, and lined with fine fibres, often built into a fork where it is moulded into the tree or bush, or alternatively built on a semi-pendent twig like the nest of the Paradise Flycatcher. Two to three eggs are laid, greyish white, often with a broad zone of darker greyish markings at the broad end; they are not specially remarkable eggs for such a beautiful bird.

Beyond that, not much is known. Probably both sexes incubate and tend the young, for they are equally conspicuous, and there is no reason why, if the exceedingly conspicuous Paradise Flycatcher male will sit on the eggs, a male Blue Flycatcher should not. However, no one seems to have proved the point. One would expect the eggs to hatch in about 14 days and the young to remain about 12 days in the nest. In Western Kenya and Uganda (where there are more breeding records than for the rest of the African continent), most breeding takes place at the height of the rainy season, April to June; but some breeding occurs in other months, which is not surprising in a waterside species whose insect prey is abundant most of the time. However, it conforms to the general pattern of most small insectivorous flycatchers in the African tropics, feeding on the seasonal abundance of insects in the rains.

The young when they fly are duller and paler than the adults; but they accompany them for some time and one may have the luck to see a family party of three or four, all flitting from twig to twig close to one another. In shade, the blue is not especially bright; but, as I so often recall them, when I whiled away the midday hours with Momo in some tsetse-infested thicket where there was nevertheless a little water, when they do perch on a twig in the sun, there's no other word for them but 'exquisite'; delicate, active, fairy-like beings.

Length 5⅜ inches, sexes alike

9 Lesser Flamingos
Phoeniconaias minor

Two species of flamingo occur in Africa, the Lesser *Phoeniconaias minor* and the Greater *Phoenicopterus ruber*. The Greater is much the rarer of the two, but still numerous, and breeds in at least two places in East Africa, and elsewhere, in America, Europe, and India. It is the least specialised, most adaptable, most widespread of all flamingos, and the second most abundant, world-wide.

The Lesser Flamingo is East Africa's speciality. At Lake Nakuru it provides the greatest spectacle in the bird world. Between a million and a million and a half may occur there at times; but I can never make it over two million, as sometimes claimed. If packed together this enormous flock would cover about 100 acres. The spectacle of their tight-packed masses, resting with head under wing, or marching and countermarching along the shore, is unbeatable, breathtaking. They are especially lovely when, lit by the evening sun, they take flight in thousands against the background of a menacing black thundercloud. They are lovely, whether individually or in the mass.

African Lesser Flamingos outnumber all the rest of the World's flamingos together. There may be six million, four to five million in East Africa, and another million or so based on Etosha pan in South West Africa; we do not know if these two apparently separate populations ever mingle. They also occur, and have recently been found to breed, on the Rann of Kutch in north-west India. All the rest of the world's flamingos scarcely exceed one and a half million; but such estimates can be little better than informed guesses. Try counting a field of solid flamingos, half a mile long, and fifty to a hundred yards deep, such as one can often see at the south end of Lake Nakuru.

Lesser Flamingos are so abundant because of a unique combination of natural conditions and specialisation to make use of these. They live in alkaline lakes whose water is actually poisonous to mammals that drink it. However, a combination of warmth, bright sunlight, and salts in the water produces a rich pasture of microscopic blue-green algae, principally *Arthrospira platensis*, on which the flamingos feed. They extract the little plants from the water by a specialised filter-feeding mechanism in the beak; and I have calculated that the Nakuru population harvests about eight tons of greenstuff per acre per annum – as much as a first class British dairy pasture. Such alkaline lakes look and taste nasty; but are incredibly productive.

All flamingos feed with their bills upside down. In the Lesser Flamingo the swollen, bulbous lower mandible is so extremely light that it floats like a cork, and perhaps helps to keep the head of a feeding flamingo steady at the right level in choppy water. In the lower mandible, uppermost as the flamingo feeds, a thick fleshy tongue in a groove goes in and out, about 11 times per second like a piston in a pump – which it is. The greenish algai soup is sucked in over a fine set of rows of hairs, which then lie down. A tenth of a second later it is ejected; and the hairs then stand erect and catch the microscopic algae. The mandibles work together, like wool-carders, to roll the masses of algae down on to the tongue. Backward-pointing fleshy processes convey the food straight into the gullet. It is a neat, highly specialised, continuous conveyor-belt process that extracts the nourishment almost free of the lethally poisonous water in which it is suspended. Marvellous – but dangerous to be so dependent on one way of eating.

Although most easily seen at Lake Nakuru, Lesser Flamingos do not breed there. Nakuru may be vital to them as a gathering ground where intense social activity in the huge packed flocks may stimulate their nuptial display. A jam-packed mass of flamingos, sometimes thousands strong, pressed so close together that the breast of one rides the back of that in front, weaves through looser flocks like some curious, multi-legged, composite monster. The jostling bodies are surmounted by massed columns of dark pink necks, and carried along by a

Lesser Flamingos

forest of twinkling red legs. Individuals in the flock perform apparently maniacal movements, waggling their bills, pointing their heads skywards, sometimes jerking the bill down to the breast as if the neck had been suddenly broken. No doubt it means something to them; but an observer must conclude that modern rocking teenagers have nothing on flamingos.

Such display does not necessarily mean breeding. Up to 1954 the main breeding ground of Lesser Flamingos was unknown. Then I found it in the middle of Lake Natron from the air; and almost killed myself trying to reach it on foot. Right out on the scorching mudflats, where crystalline soda plates and black stinking mud may reach temperatures of 150°F (hotter than you could bear your bath) the flamingos lay their eggs. Lake Natron is like some ghastly blotch of a dreadful disease on the earth's surface; but its apparent disadvantages, extreme heat and caustic soda, are balanced by the supreme advantage that, out there, they are safe from any mammalian predator. The young stay out there, in a huge khaki-coloured flock, until they can fly, and are safe to come nearer shore. African tribesmen of the Rift believe that the flamingo does not lay eggs, but produces its young suddenly, in numbers, and already able to fly.

The facts are, of course, that flamingos lay eggs and hatch them like any other bird. They make mud-mound nests like truncated cones, with a hollow in the top where they lay one – very occasionally two – white eggs. These they incubate for 28 days, with their long, drumstick red legs folded beneath them, and not, as one immortal description has it, with legs dangling either side '*Monsieur, comme sur une vase!*'; like your baby on its potty. They're odd; but not *that* odd.

The young when hatched are adorable, like tiny goslings with swollen, bright red legs, dark eyes, short beaks, and silky grey, otter-like down. Until their legs harden they do not move from the nest top unless disturbed. At five days they are much uglier, with black legs and the bill already bending. The fable of the ugly duckling applies to the young flamingo. It becomes uglier and uglier; and they gather together in huge flocks that in some colonies trample adults, eggs, and smaller young underfoot like a juggernaut. On Lake Natron and at Etosha Pan they leave the colonies and trek for miles, alone, over those awful mudflats to gather in huge herds at certain spots. Here the adults feed them; and miraculously each young one knows its own parent, which will feed it and no other. Probably they recognise each other by voice.

Ten years study of Lesser Flamingos at Lake Natron and elsewhere showed that, in a population of $3\frac{1}{2}$–4 million, only about 130–140,000 young are produced annually. If all these survive, adults must live on average 22–24 years to replace themselves. Since it is unlikely that all young do survive if follows that flamingos are very long-lived. So, when you look at a specially handsome Lesser Flamingo male, respect him. He may be an octogenarian, a veritable bird Methuselah! Its a nice fancy, anyway.

Greater Flamingos breed both among Lesser Flamingos at Lake Natron and on rocky islands in Lake Elmenteita, where the most detailed breeding studies have been done. They are more bizarre, more fragile-looking, perhaps even more beautiful than their lesser cousins. They tower over these in mixed flocks; but there are only about one Greater to each hundred of Lesser Flamingos. Their feeding method is quite different, for they extract insect larvae and tiny crustaceans from the bottom mud, dibbling like a duck. Since Lesser Flamingos can feed on the top inch of the water over the whole lake, one can calculate that the Greater occurs in numbers proportionate to the available feeding area, which is in water no deeper than they can reach by upending when swimming.

Mathematical sums do not do justice to flamingos. They are bizarre, ridiculous, specialised, endangered (maybe), archaic, and a systematist's nightmare, according to your viewpoint. But the abiding impression is of almost unbelievable beauty, and on a spectacular scale.

Length 40 inches, sexes alike

10 The Hammerkop
Scopus umbretta

Hammerkops, or Hammer-headed Storks, as some may call them, belong to a unique family found nowhere else but along African watersides. Experts are not even sure whether or not they are close relatives of the stork. It is pretty certain, however, that despite a superficial resemblance in the shape of the beak to the great Whale-headed Stork or Shoebill, (which is undoubtedly a curious sort of stork), there is no very close relationship between these two. Hammerkops do not really behave like storks except insofar as they frequent watersides and have the same feeding habits.

Hammerkops are dull brown, medium-sized birds as big as a big duck on long legs. A longish crest, partly erectile, protrudes from the back of the head so that it, with the swollen, bulging, partly flattened broad bill at the other end looks vaguely like a hammer. They are regarded with some awe by most African tribesmen, and I have never known an African molest one; it might bring misfortune on the doer. Fables about Hammerkops should be collected, as they would make fascinating reading; but even a few would take up what space I have.

Hammerkops occur on every waterside in Africa, from small streams at 8000 feet to great lakes and big rivers. You may even find one of their extraordinary nests far out in a sub-desert, by itself. Mark the place, for in the rains there will be a swamp or a pool of water there, where the Hammerkop can get the food it needs and you can get water. Any river has Hammerkop nests along it at intervals; and these nests are the centres of the Hammerkop's territory. There are usually more than one; but only one of these is in regular use, both for roosting and nesting. At dawn the Hammerkop slips out, and flies off to feed; and at evening returns, to roost within. Because a Hammerkop goes into a nest it does not mean that it is breeding. That you can only find out by more prolonged observation, or by putting your hand into the nest itself, though the odds are that if a Hammerkop comes out of a nest in daylight when you walk up the riverside it has eggs or small young.

Hammerkop's nests are desirable residences for other creatures, notably owls; but if partially broken down they are often also used by Egyptian Geese. Even were there an easy means of looking into the entrance I should wear goggles because there is no more ideal resting place for a spitting cobra; again, if a Hammerkop comes out, there's probably – but not certainly – no cobra within. The nests are huge structures, often bigger than the nests of the largest eagles; and to watch one being constructed is fascinating, for it is a work of real avian architecture, showing an instinctive knowledge of stresses and strains.

The bird begins by making an ordinary basin-shaped structure of sticks and reeds – any riverside flotsam – with some mud among it. This is normally placed in a fork on an outward-leaning branch of a big tree, but may be anything from forty to four feet above ground – or more often water. At this stage, when the base is shaped like the nest of a big bird of prey, it is often appropriated by Verreaux's Eagle Owl. Then one sees the owl sitting there, cat-like, blinking in the light of the sun, while the Hammerkop flies around, calling in an apparently distraught manner. It has to start again somewhere else, for it cannot dislodge the owl.

If no owl takes over, the Hammerkops, working together, then begin building up a hood or roof of interwoven sticks, starting from the back and building towards the entrance. The best simile I can think of is raising the hood of a pram or a sports car. Gradually they build forward until the hood overhangs where the entrance will be. The structure, which I have closely examined as it was being built, is so well-made that it will later bear the weight of a heavy man without cracking. It is completed by piling on top all sorts of rubbish, sticks, reeds, bits of cloth, anything, so that there is a mass of dead material supported by the interwoven roof. An entrance hole, just big enough to admit the bird, is then fashioned, pointing outwards and normally overhung. The bird flies straight into it; and even if you lie on top of the nest you can't put your hand in, and if you hang by a rope you are too far away to reach the back of the chamber. The inside of the chamber is plastered with mud, which hardens and makes a

The Hammerkop

permanent home that often lasts for many years. Yet Hammerkops may build such an avian palace, or even two, and not use them for breeding at all for several years.

It is often said that the chamber within is divided into sections by internal walls, but in my experience this is untrue; there is only one nest-chamber. Inside, the Hammerkop may lay four to six eggs, which hatch in about 21 days. Since they are laid at irregular intervals the young are often of different sizes. They remain in the nest for about 35 days and are left alone early by the adults, which then make many trips for food daily, and roost with their offspring in the nest by night. One advantage of the nest is that it is very well insulated; the young within, or the sitting bird, are never very hot or very cold. Some believe that this enables the female to leave the young alone early; and the pair, working together, can then rear a series of large broods. However, no one has really worked out how many broods a number of pairs of Hammerkops rear over a period of years; and from what I have seen it is likely to be low, for pairs near my home do not use the nest for breeding every year, and sometimes at all. There's still much to be learned about this uniquely interesting, common, and easily watched bird.

In courtship Hammerkops go through an amazing performance, several congregating on an open space such as a sandbank, calling continuously in their shrill nasal voices (quite unlike those of almost any stork) and mounting each other so rapidly in succession that it is impossible to tell which is male and which is female. Copulation does not seem to be complete in such displays, in which two or more pairs may join, false-copulating indiscriminately. It's the original form of communal love; but it presumably does not last long because in the end each pair goes off to its own territory and builds and breeds there.

Hammerkops feed on frogs for preference, notably the smooth-skinned agile Platanna, otherwise best known as the species used in pregnancy tests for human mothers. They also eat small fish and tadpoles; and their curious beaks have sharp edges so as to be able to grasp slippery prey the better. Frogs are most in evidence in the rains, when they themselves breed; and Hammerkops are most likely to breed themselves, especially in drier areas where the time of abundant food may be short. Despite the inaccessibility of that remarkable nest it should not be too difficult for someone to do a full study of this strange waterbird.

Length 22 to 24 inches, sexes alike but female usually smaller

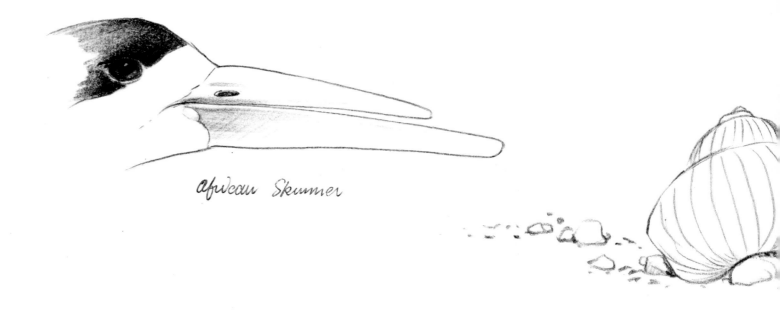

African Skimmer

11   The Egyptian Plover
Pluvianus aegyptius

and the African Skimmer
Rhynchops flavirostris

The Egyptian Plover is the original crocodile bird, the Trochilus of Herodotus, who observed in his tales about Egypt that the birds picked the crocodile's teeth. This tale has been copied and utilised since then by every pseudo-naturalist writing a book in which he can mention crocodiles; and has been expanded to include species Herodotus never saw. Sometimes they can't even get it down to species or even genus; it's just an unidentified little bird. Unfortunately, no good naturalist, from the time of Herodotus on, has ever seen a plover pick a crocodile's teeth. It's a nice fable, but that's all.

Not that Egyptian Plovers and crocodiles do not occur together; they do. However, while in Herodotus's time the crocs must have lain hugger-mugger on many a sandbank, their accessible descendants have mostly been made into shoes and women's handbags, so that in many places the plovers would find few crocodile teeth to pick. Even up to the '50s, however, there were enough crocs for curious naturalists to watch; and they satisfied themselves that Herodotus just told a traveller's tale. Or did he? You never know.

The Egyptian Plover has many other claims to interest, for it is a beautiful little bird, living in the dry season on the great sandbanks of the Nile, the Niger, its main tributary the Benue and other rivers; and in the wet season often becoming tame around canoe landings. The last I saw was on the Omo River in Ethiopia; and my knowledge acquired twenty years earlier on the Niger and Benue soon enabled me to record the first-known nest for Ethiopia. The Omo would now be as good a place as any to watch crocs and plovers together, for there are still many big crocs in that wild and savage river.

On the Niger and Benue where I knew it well this plover (which is actually more closely allied to coursers and pratincoles) was common. They were apparently permanently

resident and not, like other birds that bred on the sandbanks, temporary dry-season visitors. As soon as the floods began to back down about November they left the canoe landings and inhabited beaches and moved to the emerging sandbanks, where in due course they took up territories and bred.

An Egyptian Plover's nest is hard to find because before it leaves the eggs at the approach of an intruder the plover will bury them completely. Never have I seen an egg exposed; they must be found by sifting sand between one's fingers. Since, usually, where the plover nests there are many little depressions that look like nest-hollows one often sifts without success; and in the glare of the bright sun the exact spot from which the plover came is not easy to locate. Perspective plays queer tricks, there are no obvious landmarks, and the plover is shy, hurrying away as soon as danger threatens. I only found the nest on the Omo at the third try, having twice fruitlessly watched the bird go back on to its eggs.

As you approach the plovers perform the prettiest of broken-wing acts, or distraction display. They will also do this to other enemies, such as dogs or crows; and I have watched them trying to distract a sagacious Pied Crow, who was not to be deceived, but dug in the sand till it found and ate the eggs. Often, however, the trick of burying the eggs works; and they escape discovery and later hatch successfully.

In my experience the favourite nesting place is a spit of sand, forming a promontory a few feet above water. If an Egyptian Plover runs away from such a place it is worth watching from a few hundred yards away. The returning bird at first runs about apparently aimlessly, false feeding as it goes. But gradually, in tell-tale manner, it works closer and closer, and if you are patient, and not too badly fried on the sandbank, eventually it sits down. Wait a little more,

The Egyptian Plover and the African Skimmer

for repeated false-squatting is yet another clever distraction display. Eventually, however, the bird stays put in one place; mark the spot to within a few feet, and then it is a case of close approach and sifting sand.

The eggs, when found, are almost invariably two, sand-coloured so that they would be hard to see even when exposed, and always wet. One supposes that the plover regurgitates water over them to keep them cool; and much need there is of it too on sandbanks where the surface temperatures easily exceed 150°F at midday. They are, however, the only sandbank birds that do regularly so wet their eggs; and as far as I know no one has yet actually observed the Egyptian Plover regurgitate water over them when returning to the nest. So this is yet another intriguing waterside bird that ought to be closely watched and has not been. Maybe someday someone may prove that Herodotus had the right of it after all.

On the same sandbank, and fishing in the nearby backwaters, you will find Skimmers. Superficially a little like a tern, and quite closely allied, they differ in having an extraordinary bill with the lower mandible much longer than the upper. Both are laterally flattened, so that the whole bill is blade-like. The young birds lack this extraordinary item, having mandibles of almost equal length that can be used to pick up objects; but in adults the lower mandible makes the bill useless for this purpose; it also becomes bright red, probably used in display. Females are slightly smaller than males, but otherwise alike.

Besides its unique bill, the skimmer has a unique eye, with a slit-like pupil resembling a cat's that can be opened wide at night. They feed mostly at dusk or at night; and when feeding glide above quiet shallow waters immersing the lower mandible and closing the upper on it when something edible is touched. One recent theory is that the skimmer first cuts a line along the surface of a darkened lagoon, so attracting minute fish to the phosphorescence; then it returns and scoops up the fish in another run on the same course. This has not to my knowledge been observed in the African Skimmer; but there is no reason why it should behave any different to the American or Indian skimmers, as all three are very alike.

Skimmers often flock on sandbanks, and when approached rise to glide gracefully in arabesques and circle before alighting again. When fishing their wings are held high above the back, and their flight is altogether more leisurely than that of most terns. They are an aerial design which, having been perfected, needs no further change.

Nesting skimmers breed on the same sandbanks as Egyptian Plovers, but their nests are easy to find because the bird is dark, in strong contrast to the burning hot yellow sand; sits fairly tight; and leaves the eggs exposed when it flies. They are aggressive, too, dive-bombing an intruder as do terns. The eggs, normally two to three, are laid in a bare scrape, and are yellowish or buff, heavily marked with dark brown or black, with greyish undermarkings, less variable than those of terns but like them. They are usually laid at the height of the dry season, when the maximum area of sandbank is exposed on most rivers; but on islands in Lake Rudolf, where a rapid rise in water is not likely, eggs are laid early in the rains.

Unlike Egyptian Plovers, skimmers are not permanent residents of the sandbanks; when the water rises they and their flying chicks must leave; and they then may be seen in places far from their breeding haunts, usually in flocks. Much remains to be learned of the movements of African Skimmers; but there is no reason to suppose that their general habits differ much from the more thoroughly studied American Skimmer. With their slit-like cats' pupils and slim blade-like bill they are odd birds, nonetheless.

The Egyptian Plover, length 7½ to 8 inches, sexes alike
The African Skimmer, length 14 inches, sexes alike

12 The Crowned Crane
Balearica pavonina

'T he World's most beautiful crane!' exclaimed Roger Tory Peterson when first I showed him one many years ago; and he may well be right, though the Demoiselle Crane and the South African Blue Crane are also lovely in a different way. Most cranes are shy, wary birds, nesting in remote swamps and staying aloof from human beings. They are a group which has been described, with reason, as being unable to withstand present-day pressures from civilisation, and on their way to extinction – some being near it now, such as the Whooping Crane and Siberian Crane. Others appear still to be thriving; and the Crowned Cranes are fortunately among these.

There are either two races of one species of Crowned Cranes or two species (*pavonina* and *regulorum*), according to how you look at it. As with many other African birds and mammals, there are two races or species, a northern and western (*pavonina*) and a southern and eastern one (*regulorum*). Modern authorities have amalgamated the two into one species; but I personally consider that they are quite separate, one (*pavonina*) being smaller and much darker on the neck and breast than the other (*regulorum*). Jennie Horne, who has recorded voices of many African birds, considers that their loud bugling voices are also different enough to make them a distinct species; and they don't mix or form intermediates at the edges of their ranges, as do for instance the Defassa and Common Waterbuck. At some time in the past, when the forest extended across Africa from the Congo basin to the Usambara Mountains, the two populations were separated long enough to deverge from a common ancestor so that they could not breed together. The nearest analogy among birds are the two Ground Hornbills, the Southern *leadbeateri* and the Abyssinian *abyssinicus*, which behave in almost exactly the same way. They inhabit the same sort of total ranges as the Crowned Cranes; but come even closer to one another without inter-breeding on their mutual boundaries. Yet no one has really suggested that they are races of the same species.

This sort of problem can only be solved in the end by much more thorough comparative studies than have been done. In the meantime, the bird we are talking about here is the southern Crowned Crane, *regulorum*, which is, within its range, far more abundant and familiar than its West African counterpart *pavonina*. I well recall the pleasure and excitement I felt when I came to Kenya from Nigeria and found Crowned Cranes breeding or living in every sizeable marsh; and in seeing one evening whole flights of them, twenty or thirty strong, flying to roost. The West African bird was much rarer and shyer; and I have had the same impression when I have seen it in Ethiopia.

It would be impossible for a bird so conspicuous and so vulnerable as the Crowned Crane to survive in heavily populated African lands if it were not tolerated and respected. In the Kisii district of Kenya there is a pair about every square mile, amid a human population running to 500 per square mile when that particular count was made by Victor Burke. Crowned Cranes here nest in little swamps only a few acres in extent, where any child can reach the nest; but by and large they survive well, although the small young are sometimes caught as

The Crowned Crane

pets. They then become very tame; but can be aggressive to human beings as they grow. If allowed to become full-winged they will eventually return to the wild, but may still occasionally or even regularly return to visit their human foster-parents.

The Southern Crowned Crane has been quite well studied, the northern hardly at all, as far as I know. Probably the habits of the two differ little. They are beautiful, spectacular, and generally harmless birds except for one crime (which must be admitted) of digging up germinating grains of maize, which annoys some farmers. Otherwise they feed on small aquatic creatures, grasshoppers, and even snakes. They stalk about in swampy places, keenly scrutinising their surroundings, and strike from time to time at possible prey.

Most cranes are gregarious; but Crowned Cranes are only really so at their dancing grounds, where one may find thirty or forty together. I know of no really good description or interpretation of their dance, which involves opening and flapping the beautifully marked grey, chestnut and white wings; bounding about in a ridiculous way; and bobbing the plumed head on the end of its long neck. Both sexes dance, and they are virtually indistinguishable from one another. Dancing grounds are frequented for some time before the birds breed; but this is yet another subject which could be much more fully studied with advantage.

Pairs frequent particular swamps for breeding; and I have little doubt that they are mated for the life of an individual, which may be long. The nest is a flattish pad of reeds and water plants made right out in the open; but is usually in deep enough vegetation for the alert bird to perceive an intruder and lower its conspicuous plumed head below the level of the reeds. If you watch it comes cautiously up again, like a periscope, to disappear at any sign of danger. Nevertheless, by carefully using cover I have approached to within ten feet of the sitting Crowned Crane; and have marvelled at that beautiful head, with its clever-looking eye, at such close range.

Two to three eggs are laid, big ovals, in *regulorum* pale clear greenish blue, in *pavonina* said to be dirty white with a few brown markings, though I have never seen them. If so, another good reason for regarding the two as distinct species. Both sexes incubate for about 30 days; and the young when hatched stay in the nest for a few days before following their parents into the marsh. In this stage one may attack and possibly kill the other, like a young eagle. Occasionally two are reared, more often only one. If the eggs or brood are lost the Cranes are likely to breed again almost at once; there are several authentic East African records of two or even three breeding attempts by the same birds in a year. No doubt the young and eggs are very vulnerable to such creatures as pythons and Marsh Mongooses, though the adults are probably capable of killing or at least deterring the mongoose.

The Crowned Crane needs fuller study, like so many other species; but for most people it is enough to see them against a sunset sky flighting to their roost on top of a chosen tree, used night after night, bugling as they go. Their African names, *Mwari, Bungau, Mahem* and so on are all onomatopaeic and speak of the pleasure that many human beings get from these wild notes, akin to but different from the bugling of European Cranes so dear to the Scandinavians, their indication that the long and hard winter is past.

Length 40 inches, sexes alike

13 The Purple Gallinule
Porphyrio porphyrio

and the Black Crake
Limnocorax flavirostra

Both these birds are rails; but one is a whopper and the other a tiny dainty creature, common but elusive, not yet the smallest of rails, which are the tiny flufftails of the genus *Sarothrura*. One must sometimes give credit for imagination to those who thought up the Latin names of birds new to science, for *Sarothrura* means what it says – flufftail – and *Porphyrio* puts one in mind of the prized purplish rocks used by the Pharaohs. The name given to the Black Crake simply means the yellow-beaked marsh crow; and it's not at all like a crow except that it is black.

Most rails are more often heard than seen, with a few exceptions. If, in a marsh or swamp, one hears a loud and probably distinctive call whose author one cannot immediately see or trace the odds are that it will be a rail, maybe quite a small one with a big voice. It took me a long time, in the Bale Mountains of Ethiopia, to trace a loud 'di-deet', uttered the very instant I showed my head over the horizon, to the little endemic Rougeot's Rail *Rallus rougetii*; and it was only when the little bird displayed one of the unexpected weaknesses of this preternaturally shy family – becoming tame in the constant presence of large number of human beings – that I was able to pin it down. Likewise, Black Crakes ae Purple Gallinules can often be detected as common when not one is to be seen above or among the marsh vegetation.

The call of the Purple Gallinule befits the bird itself, for it is an arresting nasal grunt. It was this that first drew my attention to something new in a little swamp near Embu in 1947, after a season of unusually heavy rain. The centre of the swamp from which the unknown call came was covered with a dense growth of giant sedges, and water buckwheat. Several evening's watching at length produced a fleeting glimpse of the author of the grunts – a great big, brightly coloured bird with a preposterous red shield over its red beak, red legs, and with

the body largely purplish-blue and the back green. I feasted my eyes on the lovely great bird as it took a few steps along the edge of the sedges in full sunlight, flicking its white undertail coverts like a moorhen. Indeed, that's what it looks like – a giant purplish moorhen.

In most of their haunts Purple Gallinules do not become tame, and utter their deep grunts largely out of sight. However, at such a place as Lake Naivasha in Kenya they become used to the presence of fishing boats and people and forget their ancestral shyness. They then can be seen walking among the flowering water lilies, tearing off a budding head, and biting into it with an obviously powerful bill meant for that sort of purpose; or they pick off the full ripe seed-heads of sedges, which their superior size enables them to reach easily. They are much bigger than the coots, moorhens and other rails that frequent the same lily lagoons; and are often aggressive, driving these others away if they feel like it. Although, from 1962–71 at least, Purple Gallinules were abundant at Lake Naivasha in years of heavy rainfall, they have since become much scarcer, for reasons unknown. No one, to my knowledge, has yet done any very detailed study of their habits; and it was only recently that the entirely black downy young were first described. Yet another example of a large, spectacularly beautiful African bird that remains largely unknown here, though it has been more fully described elsewhere and its habits are not likely to differ from its American relative. This relative (also called the Purple Gallinule) incidentally, somehow or other manages to cross the stormy South Atlantic from at least Tristan da Cunha to South Africa from time to time. One would not think rails capable of sustained flapping flight for long, yet coots manage to cross deserts to temporary ponds; and that the Purple Gallinules appeared on that pond in Embu district in a season of heavy rains indicated that they had flown at least a hundred miles over or two-hundred round a twelve-

The Purple Gallinule and the Black Crake

thousand foot range of mountains, to take advantage of a seasonal pool the existence of which they cannot have known.

Black Crakes are much easier to see than Purple Gallinules, but one needs to be close to them to appreciate their delicacy and dainty ways. Usually all one sees at first is a blackish little form scuttling rapidly into a reedbed; but one knows there are many of them there by the constant repetition of a shrill ringing rattling call, 'rrrrr-rrrew-rrrrr-rrrew' (if you can manage that in a treble voice) which is almost certainly a duet between a pair. Black Crakes are normally found in pairs; and there may be many pairs on even quite a small pond or dam, provided that it has reedy or sedgy margins. They dislike emerging far into the open, and seldom flaunt themselves as do the Purple Gallinule, coots, or moorhens. Perhaps they are too vulnerable to attack by such birds as Marsh Harriers.

It is the rattling ringing call that gives the Black Crake its name, for in other ways it is not much like more typical crakes, the Corncrake and the African Crake, which are shy skulking, well camouflaged birds seldom seen and largely nocturnal. If I had my way I would not call it a crake at all. It is wholly black, with a pale apple-green bill and reddish legs. When it walks it flirts its tail like a tiny moorhen, though as the tail is black it is not so obvious as the white coverts of the moorhen and Purple Gallinule. If one sits quietly in a boat, or on the edge of a swampy pool, it will not be long bfore the Black Crake appears, walking daintily on long toes over the water vegetation, managing about as well as a Jacana. One may be lucky and see the pair with a brood, of tiny, coal-black mites of fluff, which run over the water weeds like excited little beetles.

Both Purple Gallinules and Black Crakes build typical moorhen-like nests among rushes, well hidden and, in the case of the Purple Gallinule, often partly roofed over, probably by the sitting bird pulling over vegetation into place as it incubates. Black Crakes lay up to six eggs, usually three to five. Purple Gallinules lay up to five. Like other rails eggs they are buff or brownish, more or less heavily marked with darker brown and pale purplish undermarking. They bear an obvious family resemblance to those of moorhens and coots. In Kenya Black Crakes breed in almost any month of the year, but the few records we have of Purple Gallinules indicate – as I suspected that year in Embu when they appeared so unexpectedly on a seasonal pool – that they breed late in or after the rains. Elsewhere they may breed in dry weather, or almost any month. Too little is known of the details of their breeding behaviour, which is in both species none too easy to watch, though a dedicated observer in a boat-hide could soon make great advances. Black Crakes probably rear a series of broods during the year, nesting again as soon as one brood is eaten by big fish, or, more rarely, grows up and leaves of its own accord.

The Purple Gallinule, length 18 inches, sexes alike
The Black Crake, length 8 inches, sexes alike

14 The Pygmy Goose
Nettapus auritus

Of all the ducks and geese of Africa the Pygmy Goose is the neatest and among the smallest, no bigger than the diminutive Hottentot Teal. An Indian relative is called the 'Cotton Teal'. In fact, it is not related closely to the true teals, which belong to the genus *Anas* and are small dabbling ducks like a Mallard; but is actually a diminutive relative of the Tree Duck, of which the White-faced Tree Duck *Dendrocygna viduata* is the best-known African representative.

Pygmy Geese are birds of lowland tropical lakes and rivers as a rule, but they can be common locally in somewhat unexpected places. They are abundant in the backwaters of Lake Tana in Ethiopia and I have also found them extremely abundant in the Okavango Swamps of Botswana, where I suspect they may be more numerous than anywhere. I first got to know them in the oxbow lakes of the Niger flood plain, those lakes left behind to become still and clear after the muddy flood of the great river retreats. They were not common there, and I never saw more than a few pairs together. In Kenya they are hard to find. On Lake Naivasha there are a few pairs if one knows where to look; and at one time there may have been more numerous than they are now, if we are to believe old accounts. They are said to be numerous in the quiet inlets of Lake Victoria among the Papyrus; yet I spent three years living near the Kavirondo Gulf and despite my searches never saw one.

What dictates the choice of habitat of the Pygmy Goose is thus obscure. I would be inclined to say that it was a bird that preferred clear still waters if Lake Tana in Ethiopia was not dull grey and opaque! Although generally thought to be common and certainly among the wider-ranging African species they cannot be very numerous in total, and ought to be watched as a species that might become endangered if not looked after. The only place I have seen them in healthy numbers is in Botswana, though there must also be other places where at least thousands occur. They ought never to be shot, for they are only a mouthful or two at best, not particularly delicious to eat, and liable to escape if wounded by diving and hiding in vegetation. The books say that, in desperation, the poor little birds will hide for long periods under vegetation, with only their beaks out of water to breathe.

Pygmy Geese are usually found in pairs or in small groups of not more than six. These may be family parties but when put to flight by the approach of a boat are as likely to split into individual couples, showing that they were made up of several associated pairs. Males and females are easily distinguished on the water; and the male is an exquisite little bird, bottle green above with chestnut sides and chest, white face separated from a greenish hind-neck by a black band, and a greenish-black crown. He looks more like the diminutive of some spectacular Eider drake than anything else. The female lacks the conspicuous face markings, and her bill is duller, not bright yellow. Both have white bellies and a white bar in the wing which immediately becomes noticeable once they fly. They fly very fast and for that reason, like sandgrouse, are regarded as choice targets by experts with the shotgun.

The Pygmy Goose

Resting on the water, they converse with one another with rather sweet, whistling calls, described as 'choo-choo-pee-wee'. Apparently it is the male that makes these sweet whistling calls, the female uttering a weak quack. Once again, they must by this calling put any observer from the far north in mind of diminutive Eider Ducks, for male Eiders emit rather soft sweet calls while the females give dull low quacks. However, the general opinion is that the Pygmy Goose, though a distinctive member of the family, is most nearly related to tree duck.

The habits of ducks and geese have often – usually in the rarer species – been better studied in captivity than in the wild state. Wild African Pygmy Geese nest in holes in trees; the old nests of other birds such as that universal provider of homes the Hammerkop; and even in the thatch of a hut. Nowadays, since the generation of dedicated egg-collectors has passed on, few nests seem to be found and the few records from East Africa in recent times are for broods of young. The fact that this bird breeds in holes in trees should make it possible to provide artificial nesting sites, perhaps nest boxes perched on slippery stilts unclimbable by mongooses or pythons, and with an entrance hole just big enough for the little goose to enter (otherwise it would be used by something else). As with some other hole-nesting species it may be partly this lack of suitable sites that limits breeding; though that does not explain why it should be common on Lake Tana, surrounded by lava rocks with abundant suitable crannies, and even more so in the flat sandy swamps of the Okavango. There are hollow trees in both places, though fewer on Lake Tana.

The Pygmy Goose lays up to nine or ten eggs in a down-filled hollow; and nothing worth while is known about the breeding habits from any studies in the wild. Studies in captivity show that the female alone incubates for about 21 days; and that when the young hatch they leave the nest almost at once. In tree sites they must flutter down to the ground like baby Goosanders in northern climates, or like newly hatched Egyptian Geese from some lofty Fish Eagle's nest. The young are unusually coloured, black above, with white cheeks and base of the neck, a black streak through the eye, and a black tail; darker generally and less broken in pattern than most ducklings or goslings.

Pygmy Geese may be to some extent migratory within the continent of Africa, their movements depending on the rains, as in so many other cases. In Sudan, they may follow the rains northwards; and they disappear from some of their floodplain haunts in times of high flood – or maybe simply are harder to find among great stretches of watery habitat, where there may be small hidden meres impossible to approach and where they are left in peace. They reappear in the scattered lakes of river flood plains as the water retreats, and that is where one may see them most easily. Even one is a delight; a dozen spread over clear blue water among water lilies are an enchantment.

Length 13 inches, male (nearest) and female

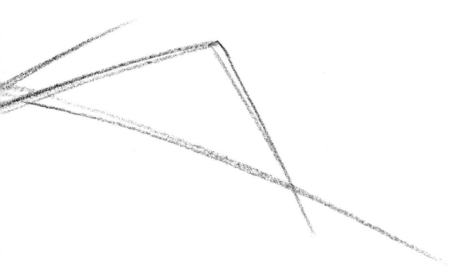

15   The Lesser Swamp Warbler
Acrocephalus gracilirostris

When I have been sleeping in my boat on Lake Naivasha preparing to watch Fish Eagles, or when I have been casting for the introduced Black Bass in some quiet backwater, I have seldom been out of sound of these little birds within the papyrus, where they must be almost incredibly abundant. Long before dawn, in the stillest and quietest part of the night, when human beings often wake, perhaps because of deep ancestral fear, I hear them singing before I drop off to sleep again. Not many at that hour, three or four in the morning; but more on a moonlit night. And at dawn, when I am rousing myself in my sleeping bag, and locating the Fish Eagle pairs by their pre-dawn calls, the waxing day is loud with the concerted song of scores of pairs, drowning out the continuous tintinnabulation of a myriad tree frogs.

The songs of the reed-warbler group are all somewhat alike, sweet rather grating burblings, for some reason apt to the waterside, and reminding one of the chuckling of wavelets or the rustle of water over stones. Yet, if one listens objectively, they bear no resemblance to any sound made by water, so that the feeling must be one of association only. All that one can say is that they seem the perfect accompaniment to a lazy, hot afternoon, when one lies in the shade of a tree and chews a straw or lolls on the cushions of a boat – though I nearly always forget these amenities in mine. On Lake Naivasha and doubtless elsewhere these little birds never quite stop singing, all the year round, and at any hour of the day. If they did not sing one would certainly not be aware of how common they are, for in the dense hushed ranks of papyrus they are not easy to see.

Parked in my backwater, in the heat of the middle of the day, when the Fish Eagles are not doing very much, I become aware of a quiet little brown bird working its way through the papyrus and searching for insects. It is largely silent, but occasionally emits a chortle of song. One can't call it in any way beautiful; but it is neat and graceful in form and movement, clinging with long toes to the upright triangular stem of a papyrus head, continually looking up and round it to detect some insect prey. Then it flits away and disappears; but if one moves a few yards and ties up again it or another one soon appears, sings a snatch or two, and in a few moments disappears. How many pairs an acre of dense papyrus may conceal I have no idea; and so far as I know no one has searched an acre of that daunting, stifling cover to find out.

The Lesser Swamp Warbler

Fortunately (for the interior of a papyrus bed is the sort of study to which one would only condemn an ornithological student whom one thoroughly disliked) one can find out a good deal about these little birds simply by watching them from a comfortable reclining position with a glass of iced beer in hand. They are not shy; and if you stay still they will come to within a few feet. At Naivasha they are used to fishermen's boats and pay little attention to them. They nest quite freely in exposed places; and it is no chore to watch a pair coming and going as they feed their young. All the same, as usual, little detail seems to have been recorded of this common and easily watched bird.

Nests that I have found, and which have been described by others, are marvels of neatness. Appropriately, they are made of the filamentous bracts of the feathery papyrus heads, each one nipped off and first bound on to the upright of two to three papyrus stems, then formed gradually into a tough neat little cup that long outlasts the brood that may be reared in it and can be collected later to see exactly how it is put together. When the outer, still transparent envelope is constructed fully it is lined with small feathers or down. In it, two or three eggs are laid, bluish-white, heavily spotted with brown. The neatness of the nest and its placement between reed stems sometimes quite high up near the flower head of the papyrus from which it is largely made is in itself diagnostic of ownership, for it is not sunk among dense vegetation. It bears the same sort of relationship to that of the Swamp Warbler, a much more widespread bird, as the nest of the Reed Warbler does to that of the Sedge Warbler in Europe.

We may assume that both sexes incubate and that the incubation period is about 14 days, as with the common Reed Warbler. Both sexes feed the young – even I know that, though warblers are not my kind of bird. The young are 12–14 days in the nest, but probably a great many nests are lost to natural predators without rearing any young. In that case one might expect the pair to breed again and again, for in the warmth and lush abundance of a papyrus bed there is nothing whatever to stop them. Yet this does not seem to be so in East Africa, for here there is a definite breeding peak in the rains. Perhaps this is associated with food supply, for the rains normally bring out swarms of lake flies. Yet such insects should be abundant enough all the year round for broods to be reared successfully, at least in reduced numbers.

On Lake Victoria the Lesser Swamp Warbler adopts a different habitat to that on Lake Naivasha, where it is almost entirely a bird of papyrus or bulrushes. Here, for reasons obscure, it is rare in papyrus, but can be abundant on rocky islands surrounded by the curious, light-wooded Ambatch tree *Aeschynomene elaphroxylon*, one of the nicer scientific names to roll off one's tongue. Why there should be such a difference in the bird's habits between two lakes not more than two hundred miles apart and both near the Equator is a mystery; but there it is.

Length 6 inches, sexes alike

16 The Black-headed Weaver
Ploceus capitalis

The great variety of weaver birds is a special feature of Africa. A few occur in India and the east; but in Africa they flourish in marvellous abundance, living in all types of country from tall forest to semi-desert, but commonest in the vast stretches of grass savanna where they find their main diet of seeds.

In the true weavers of the family Ploceidae the males are usually brightly coloured, at least in the breeding season, the female 'sparrowy', and very hard to distinguish. Seeing a flock of females one must often think them just weavers, though an expert can identify many species in the hand. Males are much easier to identify because their bright breeding dress, sometimes assumed only seasonally, just before and during the rains, is brilliant and usually clearly patterned. Most savanna weavers are yellow and black; but there are also brilliant red Bishop Birds and the long-tailed mainly black Widow Birds.

Black-headed Weavers are large and brilliantly black and yellow. They are also common, locally abundant, and associated especially with watersides where they breed in reedbeds or bushes over and near water. Along the Niger I found them commonly in the tall reeds and grasses; and near Lake Victoria I have seen colonies both in reeds and in the yellow-flowered *Sesbania* bushes so common along the shore. The nests are not easy to examine, because one often needs a boat or waders to reach them; and when wading along inhabited shorelines there is a real danger of acquiring Bilharzia.

Most common weavers behave in a similar way to each other, beginning to breed with the onset of the rains, and varying from colonies of a few pairs to several hundreds. The colonies I have seen of the Black-headed Weaver have all been large, of fifty to several hundred pairs. The bigger and tighter packed they are the more spectacular to watch; and one can often lie in the cool shade of that big green tree and watch them at one's ease, perhaps across a clear-flowing stream, or even in the lower branches of the tree itself.

As in most weaver birds the male builds the outer structure of the nest, the female later lining it and laying the eggs there; afterwards she does all the work of rearing the young, while

the male builds further nests, attempting to attract other females. One male may attract several females and sire several broods; another, not obviously inferior, none, or few. What makes one male attractive and another less so is too obscure for us.

The brilliant males assemble at a colony early in the rains and begin building. The first rains will set them off in earnest, after the heat and drought of the previous few days have left them relatively inactive. A male selects a suitable pendent twig or reed stem and then goes to and fro collecting strips of grass or reed leaf-blades with which to weave. First he attaches a woven cable of tough material to the supporting stem. Next he weaves a loop, in which he stands as a perch, and from which he does all subsequent weaving. He strengthens this, winding strips round it; and later it becomes the stiff, raised rim of the nest chamber that prevents eggs and young from rolling out even when the strong winds heralding a storm make the reeds wave violently.

Standing in his ring, the male fashions on one side a domed, nearly spherical nest-chamber, its base an inch or so below the perch on which he stands. On the other he fashions a curved entrance, sometimes with a tubular spout. Black-headed Weavers normally make no spout. The weaving is all done with the beak, pushing a strip of reed through, round and over, finally knotting it into place, with marvellous inherited skill. Young males do not have to be taught to weave; they do it in the manner born. A male may start a nest, then tear it down and start again elsewhere; or abandon a half formed ring he does not for some reason like; But if he persists it takes him forty-eight hours or so to fashion an acceptable outer envelope of soft green blades. Then he perches near and awaits a female he may attract to the nice home he has built.

One or more females appear; and instantly all the males of the colony, whether they have a finished nest ready to use or not, throw themselves into a frenzy of display. Hanging upside down from the ring or nest entrances they flutter their wings and utter wheezy rasping notes that grate upon the human ear. If the females pass on the display stops; but for a few

The Black-headed Weaver

minutes the mass of fluttering golden bodies and the attendant clamour of rasping cries is both eye- and ear-catching.

Time passes; and females ready to mate and breed appear. These stay; and one may be attracted to our male and his nice new nest. She inspects it; he perches near, fluttering his wings and wheezing, or hangs in vigorous display. If she accepts it he may feed her. She enters, and soon begins to line it with softer material, usually grass seed heads or reed fluff. The pair mate near the nest; and then she lays two to three eggs, among the most variable of all weavers' eggs, white, blue, green, even reddish, with or without brown spots. These weavers are frequently parasitised by Didric Cuckoos, whose call can almost always be heard near a colony, while the weavers can be seen frantically, and in the end futilely, pursuing the cuckoo about.

Once the female is finally hooked and has laid she is largely on her own. The male devotes himself to more weaving; and may in turn commit bigamy, trigamy, perhaps even polygamy. He spends much time in fresh outbursts of display, stimulated by his fellows or the arrival of a new female. However, if he attracts more than one mate he does not look after his wives; they must look after themselves, hatch the eggs alone, and rear the subsequent brood. The advantage of nesting over water may be to escape such predators as monkeys; but is not always an effective defence against snakes or Harrier Hawks, while a newly fledged youngster which cannot flutter back to a perch is literally sunk, or eaten by a catfish.

In such weaver birds the eggs hatch in about 12–14 days and the young are about the same length of time in the nest; the first young may be on the wing little more than a month after the first males began to weave. At this time the first fine frenzy of weaving and display is over, but one can often see nests in the same colony just made, with males displaying; others with sitting females; and yet others with females busily going to and fro feeding young. Young may be fed on insects even when the main diet of adults is seeds or grain.

Fledged young join with their female parents and form bigger and bigger flocks, which can become pests where small grain such as sorghum or millet is concerned. They must be kept away by men or boys standing on platforms, hurling stones from slings with a crack of the whiplash, yelling all day. This is one good reason for abandoning small grains for maize wherever this will grow, for the sheathed maize cob is almost immune from weavers, while if small boys are to attend school they cannot scare weavers all day.

The old nests hang there later, now dry and yellow. Now is the time to pull one to pieces and marvel at its architecture. That of the Black-headed Weaver is not the most beautifully made of weavers' nests, but it is a serviceable enough structure needing a strong pull to detach it from its support. If the young flew safely then the inside and the raised nest entrance will be crusted with droppings; if it is clean then the eggs or the small young probably fell victim to some predator.

Where wet and dry seasons alternate clearly, as in north African tropics, males may become sparrowy in the dry season also; but round Lake Victoria some at least remain gloriously golden and black the year round. Common as the Black-headed Weaver bird is, no cage canary can compare in brilliance with a breeding male, a truly brilliant ornament of the waterside.

Length 5 inches, male (above) and female

17 The African Jacana

Actophilornis africana

and the Goliath Heron

Ardea goliath

Although both these birds may frequent the same lagoon among papyrus and lilies they are very different in habit and size. The Jacana, a relative of rails and plovers, has enormously elongated toes which enable it to walk safely, treading delicately, Agag-like, over floating vegetation. The Goliath Heron, the greatest of its tribe, is a deep wader, fishing by stealth, cunningly coloured to blend with the background, and taking large fish with a precisely-timed stab of its nine-inch dagger beak.

Jacanas typify quiet backwaters and lagoons covered with lily leaves or Nile cabbage *Pistia*. Here they walk about, or run daintily in pursuit of prey. They seldom walk on dry land, though they may mount the prostrate bodies of wallowing hippos to pick their ears and eyelids. When a Jacana raises its feet the long toes curve back and close; the foot is then advanced, the toes spread, and the Jacana can walk lightly on floating vegetation where short-toed much lighter birds would sink in. It can thus forage successfully in the centre of a lily-bed, where coots and moorhens can scarcely penetrate; and the evolution of an apparently unwieldy pair of feet enables it to exploit a feeding niche denied to other birds.

Jacanas cover a large area daily, feeding on insects, small molluscs, tadpoles, some greenstuff, even tiny fish. They search intently, catching prey with a quick bill-thrust, occasionally running rapidly with part-spread wings to pursue distant prey. They seem almost always active, seldom resting, though I doubt if anyone has watched a single Jacana all day to see what it did. Pairs guard their territory from other Jacanas by running or flying at them to drive them away with loud, high-pitched nasal cries. Often, however, a large area of lilies or water-lettuce is dotted with many Jacanas feeding amicably together.

Jacanas breed on floating vegetation, making a scanty pad of weeds on which they lay 2–4 of the most beautiful eggs you ever saw. Brownish-yellow, intricately scrawled with black, they have a polish like that of a lacquered table, presumably useful in a nest almost always soaking wet. The flat pad does not hold the eggs securely; and a hippo surfacing too close or the strong wash of a speedboat can throw the eggs into the water. In stable climatic situations,

such as at Lake Naivasha or Victoria, eggs are laid in almost any month, with a peak just after the main rains in the cool dry season; but on floodplain lakes must be laid in the dry season after flood waters recede.

Almost as soon as young Jacanas hatch they can follow their parent, running over the floating vegetation like fluffy sprites. To cross a stretch of water the parent must fly; and she may carry her young under her wings. They enter beneath, their heads protruding over her tail and their legs dangling, are gripped firmly and then released when she has flown to the next feeding place. An adult may carry even four small young at a time; but as they grow they learn to flutter across open water themselves. If they fall in they can swim, but are then in danger from big fish, from which the lily-leaves they normally walk on protect them. They stay with their parents for up to forty days, and then disperse to found new territories elsewhere – if they can survive.

Jacanas are not wonderfully beautiful, but are neat and attractive in their chestnut, white and black plumage. The Goliath Heron is magnificent, not only the biggest but one of the most richly coloured of all herons. Soft dark purplish grey above, with a bloom on the plumage like that on a hothouse grape; chestnut, almost maroon, below, including the underwing coverts. The striking and killing instrument, the deadly slim head and neck, is cunningly striped vertically, to resemble reed stems. I have seen a Goliath Heron throw open its great wings to bask in warm morning sun, and the almost worshipping gesture made it a glorious bird.

Needless to say, perhaps, this greatest of all herons does not seem to have been fully studied, though it is quite well-known. They are adaptable, wading deep to fish, deeper than any other heron can; one that I know stands belly-deep daily in the swift-flowing tide over coral reefs, alone, long after smaller herons have been driven away. More often one sees them wading among lilies, advancing pace by slow, stealthy pace, to freeze immobile when a fish is sighted. Then the recurved neck stiffens, the two yellow eyes regard the fish intently along or even below the line of the beak. The fish is unsuspicious: and then – 'snick' – the great bill darts

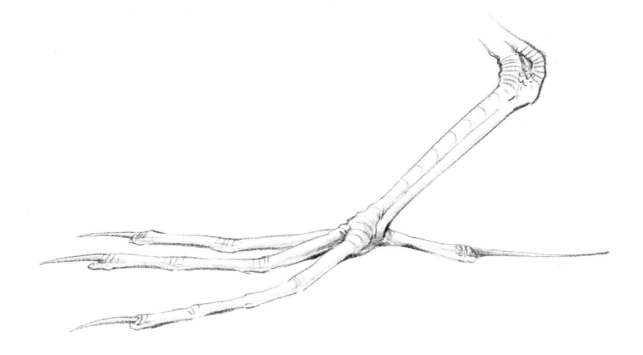

The African Jacana and the Goliath Heron

forward and the heron has it, impaled on the lower mandible or gripped between the two halves of that dagger bill.

The heron may swallow the fish then and there; or withdraw to a shore where it can eat at leisure. In any place where Fish Eagles abound a wise heron loses no time in swallowing the fish, for the kill will certainly have been watched, and the Fish Eagle will be on its way to pirate the catch almost before it is out of the water. Fish Eagles have no hesitation in pirating from such formidable birds as Goliath Herons and Saddle-billed Storks. The heron may even be driven down relentlessly until, half-drowned, it drops its catch and so loses it to the Fish Eagle; but I have also seen Fish Eagles fail to intimidate such great fishing birds.

Goliath Herons normally live singly or in pairs, regularly found day after day in the same fishing places. They roost on floating papyrus islands or in trees; and when flying from one fishing stance to another are majestic, with a slow folding wingbeat that yet carries them quickly along. One day I shall watch a Goliath Heron from dawn to dark, plotting its movements and catches accurately. The movements of the coastal Goliath Herons are controlled by the tide, not only by daylight; and inland one often hears the deep rasping croak of a Goliath Heron by night as by day.

The display of Goliath Herons bears a family resemblance to that of other species. One, or several, collect together at a certain place on the shore, where the displaying bird first slowly stretches its neck vertically upward, emitting a sort of hoot. It then bows slowly, and with its neck and body almost touching the ground or water emits a series of deep grunts, in the tone of a hippo, but not so loud. The eye of a displaying bird seems unusually bright; and as in other herons there may be subtle differences in bill and skin colour to denote the fully mature mating bird.

Nests are made on floating islands, in lagoons, among papyrus, most often in trees near water. There used to be a famous colony on Gibraltar Island in Lake Baringo where some nests were on rock ledges; but this colony has been so ravaged in recent years by animal collectors that the herons have moved to more inaccessible thorny acacias on another island, and are far less common than they were. In a tree the nest is a huge mass of sticks; but on a floating island at water level may only be a sketchy ring of dry reeds and twigs barely keeping the eggs dry.

Near the Equator Goliath Herons lay in almost any month, but in southern Africa in the rains mainly. Two to three huge pale blue eggs are laid, beautiful things to hold in one's hand. The eggs hatch into hideous little goblins, dark-skinned, with sparse yellowish down, but soon equipped with the malevolent yellow eye of the adult. Approach the nest later, when they are big and feathered, with caution, for they will strike at your face without hesitation, and woe betide you if the dagger bill hits your own eye. Exact details of the breeding season seem to be lacking, but young are at least two months in the nest. Usually not more than one of a brood of two or three finally flies. The youngster is a paler, browner version of its parent, resembling better the dead reeds among which it must often learn to hunt. As so often in Africa, there is still much to learn about one of the most spectacular of all water birds.

The African Jacana, length 9 to 11 inches, male smaller
The Goliath Heron, length 55 to 60 inches, sexes alike

18 The Collared Pratincole

Glareola nuchalis

All pratincoles are delightful. More or less associated with water or marshes, their flight combines something of the grace of the tern, the swiftness of the swallow and the airy blown leaf; and on the ground they run on twinkling feet like a small plover. They are most nearly related to coursers; and link these basically dry land birds with the aquatic gulls and terns. They are sometimes called 'Swallow-plovers' which is more descriptive than 'Pratincole', which has always struck me as especially odd.

Two African pratincoles, the Grey Pratincole which breeds on sandbanks, and the Collared, which breeds exclusively on rocks, are particularly associated with water. Strangely, the Grey Pratincole, much commoner than the Collared on the great rivers of north tropical Africa, does not extend to any south of the Equator, but the Collared extends to the Zambezi and Sabi. The two may inhabit the same rivers; but they don't mix because their preferred, indeed exclusive breeding habitats are different – sandbanks and rocks respectively.

I first met the Collared Pratincole at Ajakuta, where a single rocky island stood out of the Niger, even in flood time. About fifty feet tall, with a few shrubs on it, it was the sort of place bound to be worth a visit; and I took a fragile dug-out propelled by an expert Nupe canoeman, and first landed on it on 4 May. As soon as I stepped ashore the air was filled with hitherto unseen whirling forms, about thirty pairs being present on this rock. Yet I could find only one nest, with addled eggs, and concluded that breeding was over. The Niger flood was then rising; and soon afterwards they probably all left, for there were none in August when the flood was at its height.

I found no others in the 200-mile stretch of Niger and Benue rivers within my domain – there were no other rocks, only sandbanks, where the Grey Pratincoles led me many a dance away from their eggs by the prettiest of broken wing acts, spreading their pied wings almost at my feet. The next I saw, however, was sitting just where it ought not to have been, on a sandbank, in September. The birds had still not returned to the Ajakuta rock in January, when the flood had receded greatly; but I found them there again in April, and they were breeding then. Once more I could only find one nest, and I succeeded in taking an indifferent photograph of the bird, which simply would not come close enough. With a modern 35mm camera and telephoto lens I'd have done better.

The next I saw, 20 years later, was in a dramatic spot, on a rock on the very lip of the Murchison Falls in Uganda. All round the mighty river, compressed to less than forty yards wide, hurled itself with a thunder that shook the very ground one stood on 180 feet downwards. Yet the Pratincole was unperturbed; to it this was just another suitable rock in midstream.

Where there are plenty of rocky islands, there are plenty of Collared Pratincoles; but normally they occur nowhere else, and breed only in this one restricted habitat. They are

The Collared Pratincole

common on rocks in the Nile above Murchison Falls, and breed too on small islands in Lake Victoria. In southern Africa I have not seen them, but they breed on rocks in the Zambezi and Sabi Rivers. Why these rock-breeding pratincoles should have been able to penetrate far south while the sandbank-loving Grey Pratincole does not I do not know; perhaps because there are few real sandbanks in the Victoria Nile, or on Lake Victoria itself, while there are many rocks.

No one to my knowledge has studied the Collared Pratincole much. Like other pratincoles they are insectivorous, aerial hunters hawking flies and other such prey over water; perhaps that's what gives them a touch of swallow in flight. In some areas they migrate locally; they were absent from the Ajakuta rock in the Niger at least from July to January, during and just after the Niger flood; and also move away from the Zambezi at times. There seemed no good reason for them to leave the Ajakuta rock, for even in flood it stuck fifty feet out of the water; but go they did, and I have no idea where, though I saw others in July at Jebba further upstream, in another year.

All the eggs I found were laid in bare niches in the rock, without any semblance of a nest; and this seems to be usual. Those that I saw were greyish white, heavily marked with dark grey, making them almost invisible against the dark rock on which they lay. Elsewhere they seem more variable. The adults too are hard to see until they move; and the adaptation of the egg colour of these two aquatic pratincoles, sand-coloured in the Grey and dark like the rock in the Collared, is a neat bit of specialisation.

In East Africa Collared Pratincoles on the Nile and Lake Victoria breed in mid year, when the sun is at the zenith in the northern tropics but when it is relatively cool and moderately dry after the long rains. They lay 1–2 eggs, many clutches having been collected by the indefatigable Charles Pitman, long-time Game Warden of Uganda. He did not learn much more about them than I did; but like me he could probably visit these isolated rocks only when he could get there between other jobs, and could not even stay to watch for one day. The rocks are not always easy to reach, and may be far from shore, or in the midst of seething rapids where the chance of being eaten by a big croc makes one keep one's heart in one's mouth.

When someone does find time to watch a Collared Pratincole it will probably be found, like the European Pratincole, that both sexes incubate the eggs for about 18 days. Unlike those of the Common and Grey Pratincoles, however, small young cannot run freely about, but must stay put on their rocks, at least until strong enough to move with certainty on water-polished footing. It would not surprise me to find that their claws were specially sharp, enabling them to cling securely to crevices; but no one seems to know.

The Collared Pratincole thus remains a bird of some mystery, though common and easy enough to watch where it does occur. If ever I watch one I shall try to pick a placid stretch of river, where I can cast for Nile Perch in the evening, with a forest tree or two for midday shade, and where I can sleep at peace in the middle of the great river listening to the burbling of hippos. Wherever it may be, its *not* going to be that terrifying rock on the lip of the Murchison Falls.

Length 8 inches, sexes alike

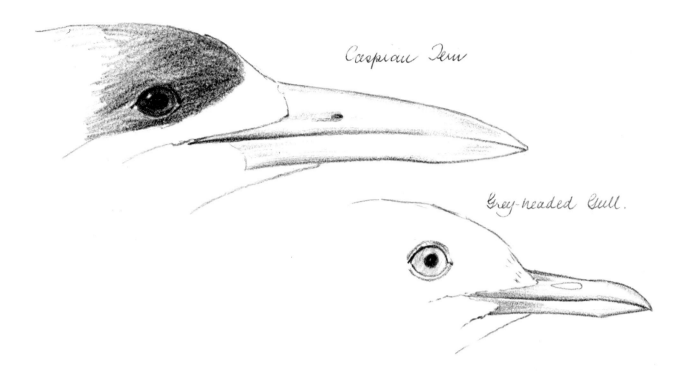

Caspian Tern

Grey-headed Gull.

19 The Grey-headed Gull
Larus cirrhocephalus

and the Caspian Tern
Sterna tschegrava

Most gulls are marine; but some are found breeding more often on inland waters, such as the Common and Black-headed Gulls in Europe, and the American Franklin's and California Gulls. The Grey-headed Gull is among these. Rather bigger than a Black-headed Gull, it will remind anyone familiar with Scottish lochs by voice and habits of both Common and Black-headed Gulls. In winter it is hard to distinguish from migrant Black-headed Gulls on African lakes; but the eye of the Grey-headed is always whitish, that of the Black-headed dark or black.

Grey-headed Gulls are the common gulls of inland East African lakes. They occur too in South America, in similar habitat; and apparently the two widely separated types are not even racially distinct. They are another link in a chain of evidence joining South America and South Africa; but it is scarcely credible that they have not changed one iota since the two great continents are supposed to have drifted apart.

Grey-headed Gulls, like many other gulls, eat what they can get; but their main diet is probably small fish, and the small crustacea that often abound in alkaline lakes. They regularly hawk over the water, picking such small prey from the surface. They also scavenge; and at flamingo colonies they live largely on the contents of abandoned eggs that they cannot themselves break. They also eat insects at times, and I have known them feed on Army Worms, a pest of young crops and grasslands. Thus they resemble the California Gulls of Utah, that saved the early Mormon settlers from disaster by eating up a plague of locusts. On the whole they are beneficial birds.

They breed mainly in colonies on rocky islands in lakes or along muddy lagoon shores; but sometimes make nests in lily lagoons among floating vegetation. Certain favoured rocks in Lake Victoria may have hundreds of breeding pairs. In the breeding season they are very smart, with a neat grey hood, red bill and legs. They build slight nests of what little material they can find, straws, sticks, dead reeds, flamingo feathers, often in a crack or hollow between two stones. In East Africa they breed in or just after the rains; but whether this is connected with food supply or with climate is still obscure. In South Africa they breed from July to November in different places.

Two to four eggs, usually two to three are laid. Like many gulls' eggs they are highly variable, from pale green-blue with a ring of brown spots round the broad end to deep olive-brown marked heavily with black. No two neighbouring nests have eggs quite the same; but the commonest are various shades of buff or brown, with darker markings. Both sexes incubate for about 24–25 days, and the young when they hatch are pale brown marked with black. They soon leave the nest and move about, and can swim well when still completely downy. However, few of these youngsters seem to survive to fly, at least in colonies I have watched. Yet the gulls continue to flourish, so they must be more successful elsewhere.

Once breeding is over young and adult flock together and then move freely from lake to lake. Their movements are irregular and not well understood; but they will appear on any inland lake in the off season. They return to breed in favourite places year after year; yet they have not been fully observed at any, common as they are.

The Grey-headed Gull and the Caspian Tern

Caspian Terns sometimes occur on the same lakes, especially on alkaline lakes. They are curious birds, with a discontinous and very wide distribution, not breeding in every place where they apparently could. They breed, for instance, in the Baltic; the scorching hot Dahlac Archipelago in the Red Sea, on a sandbank at the mouth of the Niger; at St Lucia Bay in Natal, and near the Cape of Good Hope. With that variation one wonders why they do not breed, for instance, anywhere on Lake Turkana, that great inland Jade Sea where there are plenty of fish, and suitably inaccessible islands. They were said to do so once, but the record cannot now be traced and there are no recent cases. We may yet find them there, for Lake Turkana is still partly unexplored; but certainly the easy explanation of an available food supply and a place to lay its eggs does not always satisfy the Caspian Tern.

Of all terns it is the greatest and most impressive, as big as a big gull, with a steadily measured, purposeful wingbeat lacking the airiness of most terns. At rest its powerful blade-shaped, tomato-red beak at once distinguishes it from any other. In Kenya Caspian Terns can be seen moving south down the coast in August, presumably migrants from Europe and Asia; and they may then also follow the chain of lakes in the Rift Valley from the Red Sea to Lake Nakuru; there is suitable habitat all the way down. However, we know little about their movements within Africa, except that they are mostly migrants and rather scarce. All one can say is that they are queer birds, and one cannot easily explain why they don't stay and breed in what appears perfectly suitable habitat.

I have never yet clapped eyes on a Caspian Tern's nest. I first saw them at the mouth of the Bonny River in the Niger Delta, an old slaving station now by-passed by progress. It is largely occupied by an extensive cemetery, eloquent testimony to the truth of the old rhyme, 'Beware – beware the bight of Benin; Few come out who ever go in.' I found the splayed tracks of a Sitatunga among the deserted graves; but I could not obtain a canoe to take me out to the sandbank where the birds were said to breed. No one, in fact, has apparently seen this breeding colony since 1882, when W. A. Forbes found 'a great colony on a spit below Rough Corner (the white men's burial ground)'. Well, I certainly trod on Rough Corner, and I saw the terns; but any visible sandbanks in 1942, sixty years later, were some distance out to sea. There is thus no recent account by an eyewitness to make one suppose they still breed there; but as with some other terns breeding may only be irregular. Again, one wonders why choose the mouth of the Bonny River, and not many other places.

So this greatest of all terns is yet another bird of mystery, posing a number of uncomfortable questions to those who think that one easy obvious solution answers all conundrums. Some day I hope to see a colony of Caspian Terns, for I have always loved terns above all other seabirds; and the Caspian Tern is by any reckoning the most magnificent tern in the world.

The Grey-headed gull, length 16 inches, sexes alike
The Caspian Tern (foreground), length 19 to 21 inches, sexes alike

20 The African Darter
Anhinga rufa

and the White-necked Cormorant
Phalacrocorax carbo

Both these characteristic waterside birds are relatives of pelicans, with all four toes webbed. The Darter is one of a group of tropical or warm subtropical fresh-water birds, with other species in the East and America. Cormorants, as a group, are much more widespread and mainly marine; but the common White-necked Cormorant of African waters (about twice the size of the Long-tailed Cormorant *P. africanus*) is just a race of the European Cormorant. In Europe, cormorants are mainly marine, but African White-necked Cormorants are very common on inland waters.

Both darters and cormorants feed on fish caught underwater, but catch their prey by different methods. The darter, the more highly specialised of the two, is what an American friend calls 'an underwater snooper', slowly stalking its prey behind or among weedy cover. To enable it to do so it soaks the feathers of the body, so attaining neutral buoyancy, like a Scuba diver. When, after catching a meal, it emerges, it spreads its wings to dry; and one very often sees these birds hop out on a low perch into the sun. I do not know if anyone has observed the African Darter under water, but I assume that it behaves in the same sort of way as the very similar American species. These one can watch all day from the boardwalk of the Anhinga trail in the Everglades National Park, moving slowly through the weeds looking for prey, at about the same speed as a snapping turtle; a human spearfisherman would stalk his prey in just the same cautious way.

The darter thus approaches its prey underwater by stealth. When within range its main anatomical speciality, a trigger-like mechanism at the ninth vertebra of the kinked neck, comes into play. The taut muscles of the neck are held back by an organ functioning like the trigger of a gun, or better, a crossbow. When within range the trigger is released, and – 'ping!' – the long sharp beak at the end of the snaky neck is shot forward, and the fish is seized. The darter then surfaces, throws up the fish dexterously, and swallows it head first. Inside its beak it has needle-like backward-pointing processes which effectively prevent escape by the most slippery fish;

but may also mean that a darter becomes fatally entangled in fine nylon mesh nets and drowned when trying to take a fish from such a net.

Cormorants, in contrast, have a beak with a hook on the upper mandible, and catch their prey by swift pursuit underwater. The fish is seized and held against the hooked tip of the upper mandible by the lower; small ones can be swallowed underwater but normally the bird surfaces to swallow. One often sees cormorants pursuing shoals of fish, flapping madly over one another to reach the best positions in the front. More often they fish singly, diving with a neat little upward jump before submerging, pursuing fish below, and surfacing again some distance further on. Both darters and cormorants often swim low in the water, the darter sometimes with only its head and neck showing, hence its alternative name 'snake-bird', for the thin sinuous neck suggests a swimming snake.

Cormorants have the reputation of being voracious feeders and are persecuted in Europe for that reason. They are said to eat their own weight of fish daily; and the Dutch name 'Aalschollopher' (literally, 'eel-engulfer') is aptly expressive of this supposed gluttony. In fact, it is unlikely that a cormorant's daily appetite exceeds ten to fifteen per cent of its body weight, at least in warm tropical waters; and many of the fish it takes are commercially useless. No one should condemn the cormorant without much more careful investigation of its diet; but there is no doubt that they do catch fish useful to human beings. However, I have never come across, among African fishermen on Lake Victoria, for instance, the unreasoning hatred meted out to cormorants by Europeans. The smaller Long-tailed Cormorant on Lake Victoria is said to feed largely on tiny Haplochromid fish useless for human fisheries.

Possibly because of their differing methods of fishing darters and cormorants may be commoner in clear or opaque water respectively. A darter evidently should be able to see its prey clearly to release the trigger; but a cormorant can pursue any vague shape and grab it. At Lake Naivasha, relatively clear, darters are more abundant, but at Lake Nakuru and on the

The African Darter and the White-necked Cormorant

opaque lakes of the Ethiopian Rift cormorants are commonest. However, one cannot carry this too far, because both breed even on opaque pea-green lakes such as Lake Nakuru; and on Lake Baringo, filthy-grey with suspended mud caused by erosion, darters are commoner.

Both nest in similar situations, usually in trees, the cormorant sometimes on rocky islands. Islands where they can feel secure, sometimes far out in lakes, are definitely preferred; but if none is available trees growing in or near water are used. On Lake Victoria shoals covered with Ambatch *Aeschynomene elaphroxylon* – a lovely name for a thorny, brittle tree – are often used. Usually many pairs nest together, especially cormorants. Both may breed in the same colony, at the same time; but darters often breed in small isolated groups or with herons of various sorts.

Both make similar nests of sticks and water weeds, which become almost cemented together by the birds' droppings. The sexes of nesting cormorants can only be distinguished by slight and subtle differences of the colours of the bare skin on the face and bill, and by their behaviour; but in the darter the male has the crown and back of the neck chestnut and black, the female paler brown. Both have a white streak down the side of the neck, but the male's is much whiter, and the plumes of this streak becomes elongated in the breeding season.

The displays of cormorants are not remarkable, but the darter performs amazing antics. The displaying bird crouches on the nest, its long tail raised and fanned, the black, rapidly agitated wings hanging down on either side, and the long, beautiful lanceolate scapular plumes raised and fanned to fill the space between wings and tail, shaking with the bird's motions. As a centre-piece the dark head with white throat stands out; peculiar, maybe, but eye-catching. Such displays, by building birds not yet mated, may continue for more than ten minutes at a time. The displaying bird looks completely different from the sleek, snaky, swimming creature one normally sees snooping along the edge of a reedbed.

Both lay two to four eggs, blue with a chalky covering, which soon becomes stained brown by the feet; they are frequently wetted and evidently can survive damp. Young cormorants hatch in about 37 days, but the incubation period of African Darters does not seem to be recorded. The Darter needs a fuller study, easily enough done from a cabin-cruiser equipped with what Kai Lung calls 'all the attributes of a high-class profligacy'. One would just have to keep one's eye on the right bird, which might anger the other.

Young cormorants are hideous; young darters quite endearing, clad in soft white down. When small these latter remain in the nests, and when exposed to hot sun flutter their gular pouches desperately, exposing the delicate bony structure of the bill. Later, when bigger, they are apt to leap out of the nest into the water when disturbed, and I doubt if they can often return; so one should watch carefully from a distance without disturbing them. Beneath colonies big catfish, and sometimes crocodiles, lie in wait for such casualties; and one should be careful of how one wades about among the slimy ambatch stems.

Sometimes cormorants and darters have a well-defined breeding season; in other places they breed all the year round. Both at Lake Abiata in Ethiopia and Lake Nakuru cormorants and darters have bred continuously since 1961, in varying numbers, at Lake Abiata with peaks in the rains. Yet at neighbouring Lake Shala, where cormorants breed on inaccessible rocky islands they breed only in the rains. Since these are apparently birds of the same population, one is intrigued by what triggers off breeding in one place and not in another ten miles away; and why some should stop and others go on breeding continuously until they have killed their breeding trees with their accumulated droppings and must move elsewhere.

The African Darter (bottom), length 38 inches, sexes alike
The White-necked Cormorant, length 36 inches, sexes alike

21   The Great White Pelican

Pelecanus onocrotalus

A marvellous bird is the pelican.
His beak can hold more than his belly can.
He can hold in his beak
Enough food for a week,
It's a marvel to me how the hell'e can.

So goes the old rhyme; and its author, if ribald, was quite accurate about the pelican. The Great White Pelican certainly is a marvellous bird, among the largest of flying birds, ungainly on land, but in the air among the most majestic of all fliers, with a ten-foot span in males. If fully stretched the pelican's beak can certainly hold more than his belly; probably even enough for a week, for they can fast for days if need be, though an average daily ration may be 1½ lbs of fish. Anyone who examines a pelican's beak carefully will see that it is a wonderful multi-purpose structure in itself, with an elastic pouch beneath, which undoubtedly could hold a lot of fish when close-packed.

This beak is not actually used as for storage at all, but as a specialised expansible grab-bag or landing net. Pelicans fish in more than one way; but the Great White Pelican usually fishes in groups of eight to eleven, swimming in a horseshoe formation with the open end forward. The effect of this is to act as a 'scare line', concentrating any fish in the centre of the formation, and keeping them moving towards the open end. In just a few minutes many fish, afraid to swim under the dark shadow of the bodies and the barrier of moving legs, can be concentrated. Then all the pelicans, as if at a word of command, plunge their beaks into the centre, and flick open their wings, accentuating the shadow effect. The massed beaks scoop among the fish; and some come out with a catch. Then all swim on, to repeat the process as often as need be until all have fed.

The beak itself has a long, stiff upper mandible with channels down each side and a hooked tip, which is hollow; we shall see the purpose of this later. The lower mandible is composed of two slim, highly flexible bones to which the elastic pouch is attached. When plunged into water the bones expand like the ring of a landing net, and the fish is scooped in. Then the bill closes, the water drains out as the pelican withdraws its head, and the flexible bones resume their normal position under the stiff upper mandible. Once in the pouch few fish if any escape, and are at once swallowed with a backward toss of the head. A Great White Pelican weighing 12–20 lbs, the male being much bigger, may eat 10% of its body weight daily. Great White Pelicans catch their needs easily, in an hour or two's fishing each morning; and spend most of the rest of the day loafing about on sandbanks, if they do not want to move on and have no young to feed.

They can only travel by day; and only when the heat of the day has produced large thermal bubbles on which they can rise. They normally take off about 8 . 30 to 9 . 30 a.m. and fly with heavy soughing wing flaps low over the land till they find a rising thermal. Then they begin to circle; and others see the first who find it and join them till the thermal is a slowly rising spiral of great birds, white wings flashing in the sun as they turn. They rise for several thousand feet, regardless of whether they want to travel ten or two hundred miles; and then peel off in the chosen direction, travelling in broad Vee formation, flapping occasionally to maintain height and speed, perhaps spiralling upwards again if they find another thermal. Thus they travel majestically on chosen flight lines.

Towards evening the air cools, and they must descend. Down they come to some chosen lake, wings part closed, great yellow feet spread to act as air-brakes. I do not know how far Great White Pelicans can fly in the eight to ten hours they are airborne – perhaps 200–250 miles. This poses the question of how they move from lake to lake more than this distance apart, if they do, for one scarcely ever sees them stranded between lakes. The seem to have a destination, and arrive there regularly between five and six in the evening. Do they ever travel through the night, which their aerodynamic performance would seem to make impossible; or do they travel at more than thirty miles an hour, as such big birds well might? Glider pilots cannot give us the answer for, unlike vultures and eagles, pelicans will have no truck with gliders in the same thermal, and peel off when one approaches.

Travelling pelicans may move on only every few days, though they usually move next day from fishless lakes such as Lake Hannington (Bogoria). They have less than ten regular nesting colonies in the whole of Africa, and must usually travel to fishing grounds daily, especially when they have big young to feed. When on eggs, or with very small young, the partners of a pair may change over every 24, 48 or even 72 hours. The absent birds return, usually between 11 a.m. and 1 p.m.; and at a big colony there is what we call the 'midday rush', one of the most impressive of all bird spectacles. Thousands come in from far away, first seen as little specks up in the blue, then rushing down, slipping air from one half-closed wing and another, finely adjusting direction with alternate feet, and finally slowing to land with a great flapping of pinions. Then the thing of marvellous aerial grace and beauty becomes an almost grotesque waddling object on land, though not without a certain dignity and pomp.

Great White Pelicans lay 1–3 eggs, usually two; and in about 35 days these hatch into tiny, naked, helpless pink nestlings. The eggs are warmed by the webbed feet, and when the chick hatches it is far back under the parental tail, a helpless, half-blind wobbling thing that yet must somehow be fed. Now one sees the final marvel of that great bill. The pelican lowers its head, and thrusts the bill far back under its body, so that the upper mandible is underneath. The hooked tip of the bill in the breeding season is cherry red; and it is hollow so that in this

The Great White Pelican

posture it forms a little cup. Instinct tells the tiny helpless chick to peck at that red thing; and after a few tries it is sipping some sort of fluid, perhaps digested fish broth, from the little cup.

We believe this is how the fable about the Pelican in her Piety arose. They were supposed in the days before binoculars to be pious because they fed their young on drops of blood plucked from their breast. Pelicans normally have a darker band across their gleaming pink-white breasts at waterlevel. This is actually caused by iron-staining from the waters in which they feed; but to people in the middle ages it could have looked like dried blood, while the cherry-red bill tip could look like a drop of blood plucked from that pectoral band. It's a nice fancy, anyway.

Bigger chicks become hideously ugly, clad in black down. At about two weeks they leave the nest and form into tight packed groups, called pods. In these groups they look exactly alike to me; yet somehow each parent knows its own young. Both can now leave the young and go away to fish; and when they return they search from pod to pod until they find their own offspring, ignoring all others. Then without hesitation they reach over, seize the unfortunate youngster by the neck, shake it like a terrier shakes a rat, and in this brutal way arouse it from slumber. Once roused it now thrusts its bill far down into the parental gullet to feed.

Later, any young who have survived these vicissitudes get their own back. They are then great big half-feathered lumps, actually heavier than their parents. Unerringly they recognise the incoming parent and run about waiting for it to land close. When it does they rush up to it, seize the beak, and force the poor old bird to a crouching stance. Then, facing one another, the young thrusts its beak far down into the parental throat, and there opens it, so that the throat skin is stretched, the young is fixed therein, and the parent can only eject it with great difficulty. As it struggles to feed the young may rise to its feet and drag the parent about willy-nilly. It looks specially distressing when a great big male is dragging his poor little mother about. The best comment ever passed on this was by Diana Powell-Cotton, who observed that those who found aspects of human motherhood revolting had better try being a pelican.

In time these great big young learn to fly, stimulated to practise by daytime winds. They slim down, and begin to resemble their majestic parents; practise the communal fishing movements whether there are any fish or not; and make short and increasingly practiced flying circuits of their breeding ground. Then one day they are suddenly gone, and they don't seem to go to the obvious nearest fishing grounds where their parents and others are. They just disperse widely and suddenly, hundreds of miles at a time. Those from Lake Shala in Ethiopia have been marked with coloured streamers, and have been found in the Sudan, northern Ethiopia, and Kenya, but never close by.

Great White Pelicans breed irregularly, in varying numbers. At Lake Shala the colony has varied from 3000–12,000 pairs over ten years; and at Lake Elmentaita in Kenya they bred continuously from July 1968 – January 1971, when they gave up suddenly, for no obvious reason. Oddly, although they appear grand on the wing, phlegmatic and wise on the ground, they are intensely shy at breeding colonies, and should *never* be closely approached when on eggs without intense caution, for they will desert in hundreds at the appearance of a human head. A whole colony can be destroyed in an hour by one incautious human being trying to take photographs, though a hippo wandering through has no effect. Perhaps for this reason all known pelican breeding colonies are on islands; deep in swamps inaccessible in the rains; or even (two) on isolated inaccessible mountain tops. That on Abu Touggour in Chad is the best known, 100 miles from the nearest water; and here the locals regard the pelicans with the reverence they deserve. This marvellous great bird, majestic and yet somehow lovable, is so vulnerable to disturbance that it will almost inevitably die out as civilisation invades its haunts.

Length 60 to 70 inches, sexes similar but female has larger crest

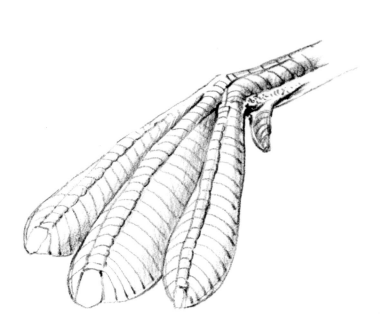

22 The Great Crested Grebe
Podiceps cristatus

Great Crested Grebes are familiar birds on many inland lakes and meres in Britain. They also occur over much of the rest of the Old World – Asia, Africa, and even Australia – with racial variations. In American they are replaced by the rather closely related Western Grebe. In fact, until pesticides and other man-made ills affected them, they were among a few really successful adaptable birds that could inhabit varied areas, from temperate to tropics, as long as there was a sheet of water and reedbeds to breed in – the antithesis, let's say, of the oddly choosy Caspian Tern.

Grebes are diving birds with short legs and lobed, not webbed feet, set far back on the body. They are exclusively aquatic, never perch on trees or rocks, as cormorants and pelicans do, and have difficulty even in climbing out onto their nests. They rest and sleep on the water, but are swift and powerful fliers able to migrate from one lake to another, and probably moving more by night than in daylight. Their flight is swift and direct, with rapid wingbeats, normally low over the water; but on migration they must often fly high over barren deserts or rocky mountains to reach some of the waters where they suddenly appear.

Tropical African Great Crested Grebes are confined to largish lakes, not, like the Little Grebe, found on small seasonal ponds or rivers. They are local and even they do not occur everywhere they should. For instance, I never saw one in backwaters on Lake Victoria in three years' residence, though their more adaptable relations, Little Grebes, were common. The resident African population is augmented in winter by migrants from Asia and Europe, notably on more northern lakes such as those in the Ethiopian Rift Valley.

They used to occur commonly on the lakes of the East African Rift, if these contained fish – as all the fresh water lakes and some alkaline ones did or do. This makes their absence from such apparently perfectly suitable places as Lake Victoria more mysterious. They ought

to occur wherever there is quiet, fairly deep water with fish and reedbeds; but they do not; and no one I know can tell me why this should be. They apparently never have been found on Lake Victoria, at least as residents.

Great Crested Grebes are very vulnerable to one modern invention, the fine nylon gill net. Gill nets are set in long lines, sunk just beneath the surface, to catch fish of a certain size; the fish swims into the net, is caught behind the gill covers, and can't back out again. Such nets are supposed to be set only at night; but no one enforces the rules. The unfortunate grebes dive after fish, swim into the net, cannot or do not back out of it, becomes entangled, and are drowned. The toll is especially heavy in such places as the lagoons of Lake Naivasha where many people set small nets to catch a household supply of fish. The once common grebes have been almost exterminated on Lake Naivasha in the last thirty years.

Where not hampered by such obstructions the grebes catch their prey by swift underwater pursuit, stabbing the fish with their blade-like bills; again I do not know if anyone has seen a wild grebe do it, but they can be watched in an aquarium tank. Little Grebes, which feed more on surface-loving creatures such as tadpoles, and less on fish, lack this blade-like bill; and the reason for the precise shape and tilt of various grebes' bills would be a study in itself. The bill shape is often a good guide to identity, especially in winter plumage.

In breeding dress Great Crested Grebes are beautiful; and in Africa they wear it all year round. The long, shining white neck is surrounded by a ruff of chestnut feathers below the head, and a couple of green-black horns or 'ears' of feathers adorn the crown. The eye is especially lovely, bright red like a jewel. I often wonder why birds eyes should be a particular colour; and I would be intrigued to know why the eyes of grebes and divers are red while those of the maritime Shag are bright green. One feels that it cannot only be for vision.

The Great Crested Grebe

Great Crested Grebes apparently pair for life; and have a very elaborate courtship, first studied in detail by Julian Huxley. In the commonest ceremony the pair face one another, beaks pointing rigidly upwards, ruffs spread, horns erected, and wag their heads vigorously from side to side. Sometimes, after a dive, both bring up weed, approach, face one another, and suddenly rise upright, breast to breast, swaying for a few moments before sinking back again. In the Western Grebe of America this is further elaborated into an extraordinary scuttering dance along the surface together. Many other forms of display occur; and in several of them the chestnut ruff round the neck and the erected ears are important.

Like all grebes, Great Crested Grebes make flattened pads of water weeds as a nest, usually anchored to some underwater growth. They are just pads of soaking wet material, but may be quite substantial, with more below than above the surface. They may be solitary, or semi-colonial, with many nests in a small area. Both sexes build; but often the female stays on the nest building while the male fetches material from round about. Weeds continue to be added, often as part of a nest-relief ritual, throughout the incubation period, which lasts about 28 days in Britain, and no doubt elsewhere too.

Grebes' eggs are long ovals, originally white, but soon becoming stained brown in their wet nests. If the sitting bird leaves the nest he or she hurriedly covers the eggs with weed, dives, and surfaces some distance away. Eggs are also covered if the bird leaves of its own accord; and this perhaps helps to conceal what would otherwise be very obvious white objects from marauding gulls. Covering the eggs with weeds is also said to keep them warm, for the soggy, fermenting mass of the nest is often quite hot inside. Probably in the tropics any such warming funcion is unimportant; but the habit persists.

Baby Great Crested Grebes are strikingly striped black and white. They can swim as soon as they hatch, and the first-hatched often take to the water to be tended by whichever bird is not on the nest – for both sexes share all nesting duties. Once the eggs have hatched the family swims around together; and if the young are tired, or when they need to roost, they climb on to the parental back and rest there, half hidden among warm, silky feathers. A pair with a family is charming to watch, for until the young can feed themselves they are assiduously tended with titbits by both parents; the male tries hard at first, but later becomes less attentive. Young in East Africa stay with their parents about two and a half months, and can be seen in most months since, near the Equator, breeding occurs most of the year, with perhaps peaks in the rains and cool mid-year dry season.

Great Crested Grebes are not only vulnerable to gill nets but also to pollution with pesticides; and have been reduced in Europe by the latter, though still quite common. The relatively solitary grebes are always much less obvious than, for instance, cormorants affected in the same way, and could disappear unnoticed while the cormorants are still numerous. One or other inventions of modern man adversely affects their otherwise wide distribution and apparent success. Since they are so decorative, and never numerous enough to be harmful, it would be a pity if the increasingly prevalent ills of civilisation wiped them out – as could happen if we do not take care of them properly.

Length 18 to 20 inches, sexes alike

Rena

23 The Painted Snipe

Rostratula benghalensis

and the Saddle-billed Stork

Ephippiorynchus senegalensis

One can see both these birds together along the edge of a lake or swamp; but if one did one's eye would be taken by the majestic pied stork rather than the little Painted Snipe at its feet, though it is just as decorative, and perhaps even more interesting in its way. The Saddle-bill is one of the six most impressive water birds in Africa; the Painted Snipe one of the oddest and least-known.

For a start, it is not a snipe, though it looks vaguely like one and feeds by deep-probing mud in much the same way. It belongs to a family of its own, the Rostratulidae, with only two species, one found all over the Old World, the other in South America. They are hard birds to see at all, being skulkers in reeds and marshy places, always well-concealed. If flushed they fly silently, legs dangling, with a feeble rail-like fluttering flight, totally different from the abrupt rise and swift jinking flight of a true snipe.

Our Painted Snipe is one of those odd birds in which the female is more brightly coloured than the male, and does not incubate the eggs, though of course she has to lay them. In the American species the female incubates as well, another odd feature of this peculiar family. Other families that have this habit include Phalaropes and Tinamous; so it's an apparent aberration of nature that has worked well in several unrelated groups. A female Painted Snipe, in the hand, is a very beautiful bird, subtly coloured to blend with reeds, but with the wings, wing coverts and tail adorned with golden-yellow spots. Males have these spots too, but they are less brilliant; and the female has rich chestnut sides to the head and neck, a conspicuous bar across the breast, and the wings green with fine barring, so that she is much the more brilliant. Hence 'Painted', for she looks almost artificial.

The biological objective of this curious arrangement between the sexes is so that the female can lay several clutches of eggs, and then leave them to the males to incubate and rear the young. Females are territorial, courting the males in an impressive display, which includes spreading the wings forward beyond the head and raising and spreading the tail, exposing the brilliant golden spots; this is also used in threat, to another female. The female utters a

growling call while in this display, and even has a longer windpipe than the male, convoluted the better to growl with. The male stays with her only briefly; and presumably she lays her 3–4 eggs, shows him where, and leaves him to get on with it. She can then court another male, lay another clutch, and so ought to multiply exceedingly – but she does not, because Painted Snipe are always scarce.

East African Painted Snipe breed in the rains; but can appear anywhere from a cold reedy margin at 8000 feet to the scorching shores of Lake Turkana. Probably they are locally migratory; but so seldom observed that any pattern is obscure. One can see several Painted Snipe on the same day, close to one another; and then go for months, if not years, without clapping eyes on another, if one is not specially looking for them.

Although the Saddle-billed Stork is actually much rarer than the Painted Snipe if it is there at all it will be seen. It is a magnificent black and white bird, standing almost five feet when erect, and as heavy as a Marabou though much slimmer and more decorative. Its most striking feature is the huge, slightly uptilted, brilliantly red and black bill which bears, near the base, a bright yellow 'saddle'. The blackish legs are adorned with a neat pink garter at the 'knee'. The sexes appear alike; but can be distinguished, and can presumably distinguish each other, by their eyes. His is brown, hers yellow. They can fly well, and soar beautifully; and one can gaze upon one with pleasure for a long time.

The purpose of the saddle on the bill is obscure. The Hausa in Nigeria call this bird 'Babba da jaka', the 'big one with the bag', perhaps in allusion to this curious appendage. Since both sexes have it, as they do the bright red and black bill, and distinguish each other only by the eye colour, it seems unlikely that it is purely a display adornment. It may possibly have a tactile function for when it is fishing in muddy waters; but that's only my idea.

Although the full details of courtship and nesting of this most magnificent stork are not known it is clearly allied to the true storks, and also the South American Jabiru, a name also sometimes applied to our bird. Courtship rituals include bill-clapping, as in the European

The Painted Snipe and the Saddle-billed Stork

Stork and for that matter the ugly but successful Marabou. Nests are built singly, on top of tall trees; and all those I have seen have been on top of Acacias. There never will be many of these storks anywhere because each pair requires a large area in which to fish. There are two, possibly three pairs on Lake Naivasha; but they do not breed every year. In places such as the Okavango Swamps of Botswana and the Kafue or Zambezi floodplains these storks are commoner; but in three years travelling about on the vast Niger and Benue floodplains I saw a total of six.

These great storks are normally shy and aloof, walking away with dignified gait if you follow them. In places, however, they become tame, can be closely approached, and are easily watched. They fish chiefly like herons, stabbing at fish with the bill; but also, at times, pace along slowly, plunging the part-opened bill repeatedly into muddy water and reeds, the action resembling the sensitive probing of the Yellow-billed Stork, which has the quickest known muscular reflex of any bird when it touches prey. This is why I think the Saddlebill's bill must have some tactile function, which could be useful in muddy waters where the stork cannot see the fish. Anyway, one can look at that wonderful bill as an object in itself, and wonder just why that yellow saddle; why that brilliant black and red; and why, precisely, that slightly upward tilt, and thin, blade-like section.

Like most such big birds Saddle-billed Storks are probably long-lived. No good continuous records exist to show how often they breed, or how many young they rear; but if a young one is reared its yearling colours are duller, greyer, generally more dingy than the adults, and I should be surprised if it became sexually mature and could breed at less than three years of age. The nests are huge flat structures placed on treetops and used again and again. The only one that has been observed for any length of time, on the plains near Lake Victoria by Phil Kahl, suggested that the breeding season might be even longer than that of the Marabou, which takes about four months from laying to first flight. East African records suggest that the season is timed to allow young to leave the nest in dry weather, when fish may be easier to catch; but other records from further South, where it is commoner, do not necessarily agree with this.

Fledged young stay at first with their parents for some months; then take to a solitary existence some distance away. Saddlebills are never really gregarious, never flocking like many other storks. They can never be common, for there are only one or two here and there. Although, so far as we know, this most magnificent of African storks is not actually threatened with extinction at present, it clearly could easily be threatened by, for instance, cutting down the nesting trees for agriculture. It needs careful watching, so that we may never lose one of our finest waterside birds.

The Painted Snipe, length 10 to 11 inches, female (shown) larger and brighter than male
The Saddle-billed Stork, length 66 inches, sexes alike

24 The Three-banded Plover
Charadrius tricollaris

Africa as a continent is remarkably deficient in small breeding waders and plovers. Compared to the abundance of small and large waders in temperate and sub-Arctic latitudes there are very few; and many of these, such as the plains-loving lapwings, are not really aquatic. Among smaller species, filling the role of the Ringed or Kentish Plovers in Europe, there are only five species of which one, Forbes Banded Plover, is not a waterside bird as it lays its eggs, not on lake shores, but on open rocky hills or, nowadays, sometimes on aircraft runways. Its nearest relative, the Three-banded Plover is, however, entirely a bird of watersides; but is not found in the northern tropics where Forbes Banded Plover occurs. Why these two little plovers, ecologically separated by habit, should also be geographically separated is yet another unsolved mystery.

Three-banded Plovers can be found along almost any lake shore, muddy river backwater, or small pond or dam, from Cape Province to Ethiopia and Sudan, and from Sea Level to 8000 ft. and over. All they ask is a small stretch of water with a muddy or gravelly shore; they even come to the small drinking ponds made for elephants at East African safari lodges, and can there be seen running unperturbed among the feet of these giants. Anyone who builds a dam or reservoir will soon find it colonised by one or more pairs. Three-banded Plovers are among those few species which have greatly benefited and increased from mankind's activities in this way.

They are quite delightful little birds, among the prettiest of all small plovers. The dark back makes a sitting or resting bird hard to see; but this plain colouring is set off below by a white underside crossed by two black bands, and the eye is surrounded by a bright red ring. They are often tame and can be watched from close range, while within a few yards of a parked car they soon ignore the intrusion, and will reveal the position of a nest or chicks in down. They can be photographed without difficulty with modern telephoto lenses.

Sometimes they breed alongside Kittlitz' Sand Plover or that lover of alkaline watersides, the Chestnut-banded Plover. However, they often have a small dam to themselves, at least during the northern summer when sandpipers and stints are away breeding in Siberia. A pair does not need a large expanse of shore; and a dam of a few acres may hold two or three pairs, especially if its shoreline is much embayed. Each pair sticks to its own area; and if any trespass occurs they run at each other uttering distinctive high-pitched cries 'Keeeet', or 'Wheet', also used for contact between the pair and their young. Generally rather silent, this high pitched call will often reveal their presence when at first unseen.

Somewhere along the shoreline they make a little scrape in the gravel or mud and add a few bits of debris or small stones. Herein they lay one to three, usually two eggs. If the plover is pretty, the eggs are marvellously beautiful, whitish, intricately scrawled with fine lines of black, sometimes coalescing to form two or even three zones around the shell. They are almost impossible to see against their dark dull background; and the only eggs I have seen that are as well or better camouflaged are those of the related Forbes' Banded Plover. Like many small plovers they are not particularly shy, and can easily be photographed at the nest, given ordinary care in placing the hide. Breeding behaviour has been quite well studied as a result.

Both sexes incubate for about 24–25 days, rather long for so small a bird. Though the sexes cannot be distinguished, probably the female incubates most. At change over one approaches, whistling occasionally; the other rises and leaves. I doubt if anyone has watched them through the night, but they are quite active at night, and there seems no reason why they should not change over then too. Still plenty left to learn, as usual.

New-hatched young can leave the nest at once and run with one or other parent. They are hard to see unless they move, but a little patience will soon reveal them; they will run to and be brooded by a whistling parent. In suitable conditions, or if the first clutch is for some reason

The Three-banded Plover

lost, more than one brood per year may be reared. If they survive, the young remain with the parents for more than a month, gradually becoming independent and running about more freely. In due time they must find somewhere else to go because the old birds will remain in their territory, if both survive. One never sees flocks of Three-banded Plovers, so we assume that young can soon find an unoccupied stretch of shoreline, and mate and breed themselves.

A large number of East African records shows that they breed in many months, but with a peak in and just after rainy seasons. Further south, in Rhodesia, the peak is definitely in the dry season. Breeding in any area should be at a maximum when the eggs are unlikely to be drowned by floods or washed out by very heavy rain and in Eastern Kenya the cool dry season, May to July, is preferred. As the young mature, the shoreline of the pond or dam they inhabit should be receding inch by inch, exposing each day a little more soft mud, no doubt rich in insect larvae; but I doubt if anyone has measured exactly how much new feeding ground becomes available to a pair each day or week.

It is interesting to compare this tendency to dry season breeding in a waterside bird with that of Forbes Banded Plover, which breeds in the height of the rains on its barren naked rock sites. In the only place where it has ever been studied in any detail (by myself in Nigeria many years ago) all nests found were on naked rock slabs, the only really dry expanse for miles at the season – May to August – when I found eggs. Available food supply is usually advanced as the main factor controlling breeding seasons; but would be hard to prove for either of these small plovers. Again, it seems very odd that Forbes Banded Plover does not breed in the same area, south of the Equator, seeing that there could be no conceivable competition for nesting space or food. There are plenty of suitable rocks in Zambia. These plovers may be closely related to one another; but are totally different in habit, though each is very ornamental and among the prettiest of small plovers.

Whether one wants to indulge in this sort of relatively advanced speculation or not, one can always enjoy watching a pair of Three-banded Plovers along a dam shoreline. Often one can do it in great comfort and ease, from a car parked in the shade of one of those big trees, or a comfortable chair. To photograph them at the nest one needs a hide; and must then sweat it out in the hot sun of an open shore for a few hours. However, the reward is a close-up view of one of the most delightful of all African waterside birds, an ornament to its habitat, epitomising the charm of the waterside as a whole.

Length 7½ inches, sexes alike